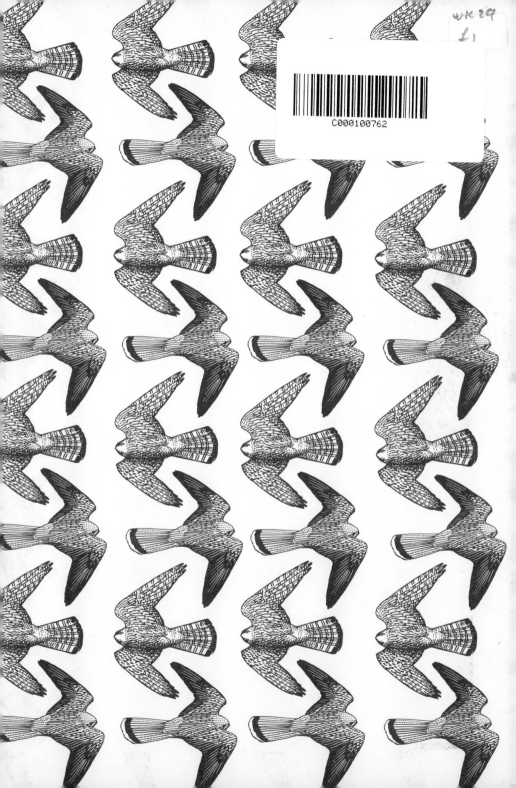

# FALCONS

# FALCONS

## •ANDREW VILLAGE•

with illustrations by
DARREN REES

**Whittet Books**

*Endpaper illustration:* Kestrels

*Title page illustration:* Peregrine over the Lleyn peninsula

First published 1992
Text © 1992 by Andrew Village
Illustrations © 1992 by Darren Rees
Whittet Books Ltd, 18 Anley Road, London W14 0BY

Design by Richard Kelly

**British Library Cataloguing-in-Publication Data**

Village, Andrew
    Falcons. – (British natural history)
    I. Title   II. Series
    598.918

    ISBN 1873580002

Typeset by Litho Link Ltd, Welshpool, Powys, Wales
Printed and bound by Biddles of Guildford

# Contents

# Preface

This book is about the falcons that breed in Britain: the peregrine, merlin, kestrel and hobby. Although I have tried to give equal space to all four species, the sharp-eyed reader will notice a definite bias towards kestrels. This perhaps reflects the fact that I studied kestrels for fourteen years but, personal preferences aside, it is also because there is much more information about kestrels than the other three species. This is particularly true when it comes to data collected by ringing, because three times more kestrels have been ringed in Britain than the other falcons combined. I have used examples from the other species whenever possible, but often the only detailed information comes from kestrels.

I would like to thank the many researchers whose work I have drawn on to fill the gaps in my knowledge of peregrines, merlins and hobbies. I have tried to mention them by name where appropriate, but I hope those who remain anonymous will forgive the omissions.

*Andrew Village*
*January 1992*

# What makes a falcon a falcon?

Falcons eat meat. This meat comes in the form of mammals, birds, reptiles and insects, which tend to resent being eaten and try to avoid capture. The anatomy and behaviour of falcons are adapted to counter this reluctance on the part of their prey and thus make the business of getting food as easy as possible. All falcons are built to a common plan that has been modified by the particular lifestyle of each species.

Falcons share their carnivorous habits with other birds of prey such as owls, vultures, eagles and hawks. Birds of prey are often called 'raptors' from the Latin word meaning 'seize and carry away', which is what they usually do with their food. Owls are specialized night-hunters, but the rest are mostly diurnal (active during the day), and they are more closely related to falcons.

The similarity of their food and general habits gives raptors several common features which set them apart from other birds. Their eyesight is excellent. The large, forward-set eyes give binocular vision that enables them to find their prey easily and then to judge accurately the distance over which they will have to attack it. Raptors also have powerful, grasping talons and sharp claws. Three toes point forward and a fourth points backwards, forming a deadly vice with which to hold prey.

The hooked beak is used for tearing flesh into small pieces, something that raptors do with chilling efficiency. The victim is held in those strong talons, the hook in the beak is driven into the flesh, which is then cut with a powerful bite or pulled apart using strong neck and back muscles. This simple technique allows a toothless bird to dismember a carcass more than half its size in a matter of minutes. The process can be rather messy, so raptors have a fleshy cere (bare patch of skin) around the beak, which helps to prevent feathers being dipped into all that blood and gore.

Most raptors show 'reversed sexual size-dimorphism', an acute case of jargon that simply means the female is bigger than the male, the reverse of the usual case in birds. In raptors this seems to be related to the nature of their food, which comes in neat carcass form and can be carried to the nest. The male can therefore feed his mate while she incubates and broods the chicks. For reasons that are not altogether clear, this division of labour

Reversed Sexual Size-dimorphism
Can be useful

seems to favour large females and/or small males. In addition, the extent of the dimorphism varies with the type of prey eaten. The raptors with the biggest size-difference between the sexes are those that feed on fast, agile prey such as birds, while species that feed on slow-moving prey, such as mammals, have sexes of similar size. Where food cannot be carried easily, as in carrion-feeding vultures and condors, the sexes share the jobs equally and they are the same size.

All raptors fly, but some fly more powerfully than others. Larger species have long, broad wings and rely on soaring to search for prey on the ground. They are loath to flap their wings more than they have to, and usually wait for hot-air thermals to give them lift. Forest dwellers have broad, rounded wings and long tails that give the manoeuvrability necessary to fly fast through dense vegetation. Smaller raptors that live in open habitats tend to have narrow, pointed wings for powerful chases and high-speed dives.

### The falcon blueprint
In addition to these typical features, falcons have characteristic anatomy and behaviour that distinguishes them from other raptors. Unlike most

raptors, falcons kill their prey by biting, usually at the back of the neck near the base of the skull. To help them do this they have a projection on the upper mandible that fits into a notch on the lower. This 'tomial tooth' is not a tooth at all, but a serration of the beak that has evolved independently in shrikes, which also kill by biting. Anyone who has handled wild falcons knows that you have to avoid not only the needle-like claws, but also the mobile razor at the front of the head! Being able to despatch prey quickly enables falcons to take relatively large prey compared with hawks that have to grapple with their claws and hang on until the victim stops squirming.

*Head of a peregrine, showing the 'tomial tooth'.*

Most falcons live in open country, so they have narrow, pointed wings and powerful flight muscles. This gives them speed in powered flight and the agility to catch prey in rapid chases or dives, though the price paid for speed is some loss of manoeuvrability compared with forest hawks. The pointed wings are often cited as the best way of distinguishing falcons from other birds of prey, particularly when they are seen in silhouette high in the sky.

As well as differences in structure, falcons also have distinctive features to their physiology and behaviour. For example, they moult their flight feathers in an unusual order, starting in the middle of the primaries, and working inwards and outwards simultaneously. This pattern, which is found in other Falconids (falcon-like raptors), compares with the more conventional order in other raptors of working from the inner primary outwards. Another distinguishing feature of falcons is the colour of their eggs, which are tinged with a reddish-brown pigment called protoporphyrin, related to haemoglobin (the red pigment in blood). The depth of colour and patterning is highly variable, even within species, which has made falcon eggs particularly prized by collectors. There are also common behaviourial features, such as the lack of nest building (shared with owls), distinctive calls or displays and bobbing the head when nervous.

These features (together with some rather obscure details of anatomy) define the falcons as a distinct group of birds of prey that are fairly closely related to one another. How are they related to other birds of prey?

## The falcon family tree

Falcons are such familiar raptors that they have given their name to the scientific order that includes all 292 species of diurnal raptor — the 'Falconiformes'. This order consists of the accipiter family (a mixed bunch of 233 species that embraces hawks, buzzards, Old World vultures and eagles), the cathartid vultures (seven species from the New World) and such oddballs as ospreys and secretary birds that have families all to themselves because they cannot be fitted in anywhere else. The remaining family is the 'Falconids', a group of 60 or so species that includes the caracaras and and forest falcons of South America, the pygmy falcons and falconets of Africa and Asia and the true falcons of the genus *Falco*. The latter comprises 38 species that include the four falcons that breed in Britain: the peregrine, merlin, kestrel and hobby.

The evolution of raptors is complex and hotly disputed, and no one is really sure where the falcons came from. The latest studies, based on analysis of DNA, suggest that the raptors' closest relatives are probably waders, storks and seabirds. The fossil evidence shows that diurnal raptors may have arisen some 40 million years ago, with the Falconids being the most recent and specialized group. The variety of Falconids in South America, which has caracaras, forest falcons and true falcons, suggests this continent may have been important in the story of their evolution.

This book is about the four British falcons, but before describing them in detail it is worth looking at how the falcon blueprint has been adapted within the other species of the genus.

# The Mauritius kestrel — coming back from the brink

*In the 17th century, when Dutch sailors discovered the island of Mauritius in the Indian Ocean, it was covered in dense tropical forest. Mauritius is small (60 × 40 km/37 × 25 miles) and over 1,000 km/625 miles east of Madagascar, and this isolation has encouraged the evolution of many unique plants and animals. The most* famous is probably the dodo, which rapidly succumbed to the attention of the hungry sailors. But there were many other species that were adapted to the native forests, and were bound to suffer as humans 'tamed' the island. In the 200 years since the mid 1700s, 98 per cent of the native forest has been cleared to make way for tea, sugar cane and commercial woodlands. The colonists also brought with them animals such as deer, rats and monkeys, as well as the diseases they carried.

The effect on the wildlife was devastating, not least on the Mauritius kestrel. It feeds mainly on geckoes and small birds that live in the forest, and these have disappeared with the habitat. The introduced crops are vulnerable to insects, so large amounts of pesticides are used on the island. To make matters worse, the inhabitants of the island blamed the kestrel for taking chickens, so birds were frequently shot or their nests destroyed. By the early 1970s the kestrels were about to go the way of the dodo and it was thought there were only six birds left alive. Something had to be done.

One option was to move the birds to nearby Réunion Island, where they might be less disturbed. Similar transfers have helped endangered Seychelles kestrels, but they were more abundant than the Mauritius species and there was no guarantee things would be any safer on the new island. It was decided to take some birds into captivity to try and form a breeding colony.

At first things went badly. In seven years the four pairs in captivity produced only one surviving chick, and that died within a year or so. Breeding success in the wild continued to decline, so in 1980 the team began to remove eggs from wild clutches and hatch them in incubators. This greatly improved the hatching and fledging rates per egg, and helped the team to gradually learn how to get the birds to breed in the aviaries. To date, around 90 birds have been bred in captivity and over 100 reared from eggs taken from the wild. Nearly 200 kestrels have been released on the island, and by 1991 there were some 30 breeding pairs. Although the future for the kestrel looks brighter than it did twenty years ago, there is still little forest left for them on the island. The released birds have adapted remarkably well to some of the man-made habitats on the island, but there is still an urgent need to preserve patches of suitable forest for them. Mauritius kestrels are by no means safe yet, and this is one case where staying in the forest is the only way to ensure they get out of the woods!

# Falcons around the world

Although all the falcons are sufficiently similar to be classed in the same genus, some species are more closely related than others. The features commonly used to group species within the falcon genus are size, the relative lengths of wings, tail and toes and the degree of sexual dimorphism. All these features are related to the type of food eaten. This is not just because big falcons tend to eat big prey, but also because species eating fast, agile prey tend to have narrower wings and shorter tails (for more rapid and manoeuvrable flight), longer toes (for easier grabbing of prey in flight) and a bigger size-difference between the sexes, than species that eat slow-moving prey.

The genus *Falco* shows typical examples of how the same basic structure can be modified by selection that tends to favour characteristics suitable to a particular habitat and lifestyle. This is called 'adaptive radiation': and may be the result of an ancestral species diverging into new forms as it encounters new conditions. Some of the specializations in falcons have made them become more like other raptors, and this is termed 'convergent evolution', the same solution evolving to fit the same problem in totally unrelated species. For example, Mauritius kestrels have become adapted to life in dense forest, and now have rounded wings that resemble those of raptors such as sparrow hawks that are more usually associated with forest.

These processes of evolution make it difficult to decide how to organize the falcons into related groups. Do species resemble each other because they are closely related (that is, they have a recent common ancestor), or because they happen to live similar lives? Whichever way we divide the falcons, there are always a few species that don't seem to fit, and some species that could go virtually anywhere. Most taxonomists recognize four obvious groups and about half a dozen isolated species:

THE KESTRELS. The kestrel we are familiar with in Britain is one of 13 species found throughout the world. These small falcons are adapted to hunting a wide variety of prey that they catch on the ground, and many search by hovering. Some scientists think that a kestrel-like species may have been the ancestor of all the falcons, though present-day kestrels have evolved their own specializations. Most kestrels have brown plumage, and in several species the sexes look quite different, which is unusual in falcons. The sexes are roughly similar in size, which is associated with their rather slow-moving prey. The group includes the smallest falcon, the Seychelles kestrel (a feather-weight at around 80 g/3 oz) and the rarest — the Mauritius kestrel. Both these species live on isolated islands in the Indian Ocean. The Mauritius kestrel is adapted to hunting lizards in dense forests and has developed rounded, accipiter-like wings. The destruction of its forest home, and the widespread use of chemicals, has left this unusual bird teetering on the verge of extinction.

*The gyrfalcon is the largest falcon.*

THE HOBBIES. These are small, aerial-feeding species that are the acrobats of the falcon world. They are almost swift-like in appearance, with very narrow wings and short tails. This group includes four similar species of hobby that live in Europe, Africa, Asia and Australia, plus the red-footed falcons and two colonial-nesting species, Eleonora's and sooty falcons. These last two species nest mainly on offshore islands in the Mediterranean and Red Sea. They feed their young on migrating songbirds that rest on these islands in early autumn, and for this reason have a late breeding season that coincides with this unusual abundance of food.

THE GREAT FALCONS. These large falcons are adapted to take prey near the ground in open areas such as deserts or tundra. The largest is the gyrfalcon (a hefty 1.7 kilos/3.8 lbs), which is found throughout the Arctic and feeds on willow grouse and hares. Also in this group are sakers, the desert falcons used by Arab falconers, their close relatives the laggar and lanner, and possibly two Australian species, the black and grey falcons.

THE PEREGRINES. This select group comprises the peregrine and the Barbary falcon, which may be two forms of the same species. They fall somewhere between the great falcons and hobbies, taking large aerial prey and being fast, manoeuvrable fliers. They are among the most size-dimorphic falcons, females being some 15 per cent larger than males. The falconer's name for male peregrines is 'tercel', from the French for 'a third', which perhaps slightly exaggerates the size difference!

ODDS AND ENDS. This leaves seven species that do not fit any of the above categories. The merlin is clearly a typical small falcon, but defies grouping with kestrels or hobbies, so it has to stand alone. Although it feeds mainly on birds, it is nearer in shape to the kestrels than the hobbies and fits neither group easily. Red-headed falcons live in Africa and India, and have been linked with the kestrels. However, they are highly dimorphic and have long toes, suggesting they are more specialized bird-eaters. The Australian brown falcon is a strange, rather buzzard-like falcon that almost deserves its own genus. The remaining four species, the New Zealand, bat, orange-breasted and Aplomado falcons seem to lie somewhere between hobbies and peregrines. Some taxonomists think they may be related to one another, though the evidence is rather scant.

This ends our lightning tour of the falcons. They tend to be at the smaller end of the scale, as raptors go, but nonetheless show a considerable range of size and habits. Although most are birds of open country, a few have adapted to forest life and converged with accipiters. Some open-country species have adjusted well to the way humans have cleared forests for agriculture, and a few have even colonized towns and cities. Between them, falcons exploit all kinds of animals for food, ranging in size from termites to large hares. The genus is also extremely widespread, occurring on all continents (except Antarctica) and many isolated islands. By any standards, the falcon blueprint has proved to be both highly adaptable and successful.

*Aplomado falcon.*

# Falcon on the fist

Falcons have held a powerful fascination for humans for thousands of years. Having a falcon on your fist does strange things to the ego: emotions surface that are not aroused by parrots or chickens. Maybe it's because both man and bird are predators at the top of their food chains. Or perhaps the attraction lies in the aloofness and intractability of a bird that can be controlled but never fully domesticated. Then again it may be the ever-present possibility that a nervous falcon might tear off the end of your nose if you get too careless!

The peregrine is a favourite bird of falconers.

No one knows for certain how or when humans started hunting with birds of prey. The earliest documented record is a carved stone slab from Assyria, dated about 700 BC, which shows a man holding some kind of hawk. Most people agree that hawking probably originated independently in several parts of the Middle and Far East as early as 2,000 BC. Falcons were probably eaten as food originally, as indeed they still are in some parts of the world where young chicks are considered a delicacy. Perhaps some subversive tribesman decided to rear his peregrine chick rather than eat it, or give an injured adult the same sympathetic treatment. Whatever the origins, people soon found they could use hawks to catch food, and falconry was well established from Arabia to Japan well before the birth of Christ.

The Greeks and Romans were not into hawking, but it caught on in a big way in Western Europe. Falconry has been practised in Britain since Saxon times, but it received an added impetus when all those gallant knights came back from the Crusades. This helped spread Arab know-how into Europe, and Emperor Frederick II of Hohenstaufen, a real fanatic, imported hawks and trainers from Arabia. In 1250 he wrote a massive tome on the art of falconry which is still used today.

By this time, falconry had status attached to it and was largely the sport of the rich. Although raptors other than falcons were flown, such as eagles and goshawks, peregrines were always a favourite. This was partly due to their spectacular hunting prowess and partly because they are relatively docile and easily trained. Peregrines were reserved for the upper classes, merlins were considered a 'lady's hawk' while poor old kestrels were deemed fit only for the proletariat. There were strict penalties for raiding peregrine eyries, which became prized properties from the 13th century onwards. It is in this period that references are found in writings to peregrine nesting-cliffs, some of which are still used today.

The main falcons flown were gyrfalcons, peregrines and sakers. In Europe, the height of the art was to fly these at large birds such as herons, kites and cranes. The object with herons was to release the falcon from the fist at a high-flying quarry, which would then begin to climb in an effort to escape. The result would be a spectacular 'ringing flight', in which the birds circled upwards while covering long distances overland. The hawkers would often have to be on horseback to follow properly.

And then along came the gun. Sporting man found he could kill game more effectively than hawks, which suddenly became a rival rather than a partner. From the mid 1700s, falconry gave way to game shooting, and wild falcons were slaughtered in order to protect gamebirds so humans could slaughter them too. Falconry had all but died out over much of Europe by the early part of this century. However, a small but enthusiastic band kept the sport going, and since World War II it has become increasingly popular, with over 20,000 devotees worldwide.

## Falconry today

Strictly speaking, the term 'falconry' should be reserved for the flying of falcons; those using hawks are more correctly called 'austringers' (another useful fact for your next game of Trivial Pursuits). Several species of falcon are used by falconers today, but the most prized are still the larger species such as gyrfalcons, peregrines and sakers.

Most European falconers rear 'eyasses' (young chicks) that are taken from the wild or bred in captivity. The sport is strictly controlled, and falconers need special licences to keep birds, to take wild falcons and to fly them at prey. Training falcons takes a long time, and involves getting the bird accustomed to flying to the fist, then to stooping (diving) at a lure and finally to attacking prey. Falcons that do the right thing are rewarded with a juicy titbit of meat and, like most noble creatures of the wild, will soon sell their souls for the entrails of a day-old chick! The trainer keeps his bird on a strict diet to control its weight: overfeeding makes birds reluctant to hunt but underfeeding can make them weak fliers. Keeping a falcon's weight in narrow limits is easier for larger birds, so kestrels, though usually treated as beginners' birds, can be difficult to keep in flying condition.

For most falconers the attack is more important than the kill — they look for the exciting chase or the dramatic stoop. Falcons may be trained to 'wait on', soaring overhead until prey is flushed, or released from the fist when prey is seen. Peregrines can be flown from the fist at slower birds such as rooks, crows or gulls, but they can only catch fast gamebirds if they are already 'waiting on' before the prey is flushed. The traditional quarry for female peregrines are red grouse, flushed from cover by a trained dog such as a pointer or setter. Some male peregrines can catch grouse, but they are mostly flown at partridges.

Falcons don't have to be big to provide exciting sport. Merlins have always had a dedicated band of enthusiasts who believe that what they lack in quantity they more than make up in quality. They were often trapped as full-grown birds and kept only during the summer, but the licensing laws make this impossible now. The classic way to fly merlins is after skylarks — the close match of aerial abilities result in prolonged 'ringing' flights, the falcon climbing above the rapidly rising lark.

# Arabian flights

Falconry in Arabia is quite different from that usually practised in Europe or America. In the desert, hawking was not just a sport but an important way of supplementing an otherwise meagre diet. Falcons were flown by rich and poor alike and hunts still provide an important bridge across social divides. Falcons are trapped during autumn migrations in Pakistan, Iran, Afghanistan and on the Arabian Peninsular. Most are immatures, sakers making up around 70 per cent of the 3,000 or so falcons flown in the peninsular each year. Sakers are better adapted to the hot temperatures of the interior than are peregrines, which tend to be used around the Gulf coast.

The falcons are trained quickly to allow them to be handled yet still maintain their aggression. Arab falconers delight in the more functional aspects of the kill: birds are flown from the fist directly at prey and are expected to chase the quarry and bind to it, bringing it to ground. The usual quarry are Houbara bustards or the smaller but similar-shaped stone curlew. Falcons are flown during winter and many are released in spring, ready to return to their breeding areas.

Arabian falconry has a long tradition, woven into the fabric of the culture and even sanctioned by the Qu'ran. Today, the camel transport is replaced by four-wheel-drive vehicles, and hunts have tended to become the show-pieces of those made wealthy by oil revenues. However, there is a real concern to preserve this way of life, and this has led to the setting up of several well funded raptor centres and research into conserving the endangered prey species.

# British falcons

Four species of falcon breed in Britain: the peregrine, merlin, kestrel and hobby. Other falcons that occasionally turn up on our shores are gyrfalcons, American and lesser kestrels and red-footed falcons, though visits are sufficiently rare to have twitchers grabbing their binoculars and diving for the nearest bus. The four natives all differ in appearance and habits, and co-exist by exploiting different lifestyles (or 'niches').

THE PEREGRINE (*Falco peregrinus*). The peregrine is the largest British falcon, females being around 47 cm (19 in) bill to tail, males 43 cm (17 in). They are powerful fliers, renowned for their spectacular dives at prey which may reach speeds of over 160 kph (100 mph). Peregrines are heavy

A Guide to the Falcons of the British Isles

for their size and the wings are broad for a falcon but typically pointed. The sexes have similar plumage and can be difficult to tell apart unless seen together, when the male's smaller size is more obvious. Adults have blue-grey upper-parts and white or cream under-parts, with varying degrees of horizontal barring. A noticeable feature on the head is the dark 'moustache' below the eye, which varies between individuals and may be as unique as our fingerprints. The cere and legs are bright yellow.

First-year birds are much browner all round, with buff fringes to their feathers. The moustache is less obvious than in adults because the surround is a dirtier white and heavily marked. The legs and cere change colour as the birds develop, from grey in nestlings through greenish yellow in juveniles to the full adult yellow.

THE MERLIN (*Falco columbarius*). Merlins are the midgets, females averaging about 28 cm (11 in) in overall length and the males some 9 per cent less. Although aerial predators, they are shaped somewhere between a kestrel and a hobby, with a long tail relative to the wings. They are fast fliers, often seen dashing along close to the ground. Unlike peregrines, the adult males and females have quite different plumage. Males are blue-grey above with white or cream undersides that are streaked with rufous. Females are altogether more dowdy and resemble juveniles: dark brown above and heavily streaked below. Neither sex has a noticeable moustache, the side of the head being streaked like the undersides.

THE KESTREL (*Falco tinnunculus*). Kestrels are about the size of hobbies (33-4 cm/13-14 in for both sexes), but with much longer tails, shorter wings and slightly less size-difference between the sexes. They primarily eat rodents, and rarely catch prey in the air. The kestrel is the only British bird of prey that frequently hovers, making it instantly recognizable, even in the brief glance you sometimes get from the window of a car speeding down a motorway. Like merlins, the sexes have distinct adult plumage. Males have grey heads and tails, pinkish-red backs with black spots and white, spotted undersides. Females are less flamboyant, being brown and barred above and off-white with streaks below. In some adult females the tail and rump are grey or grey-brown, but always barred, unlike the males. There is a slight moustache in both sexes, most obvious in the males. Juveniles tend to look like adult females, but are browner and more heavily marked all round.

THE HOBBY (*Falco subbuteo*). A much smaller, slimmer version of the

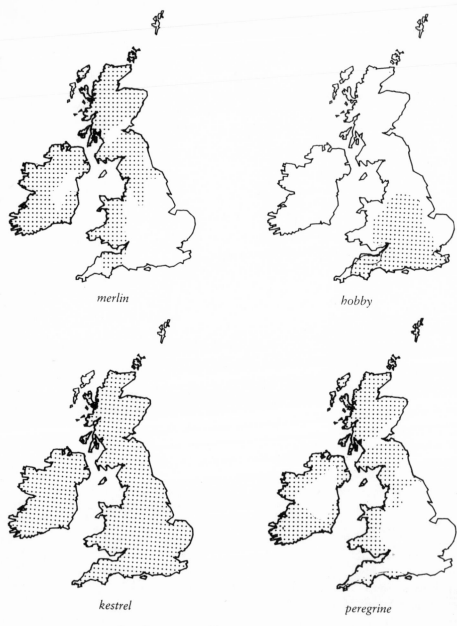

*merlin*

*hobby*

*kestrel*

*peregrine*

*Breeding ranges of falcons in the British Isles.*

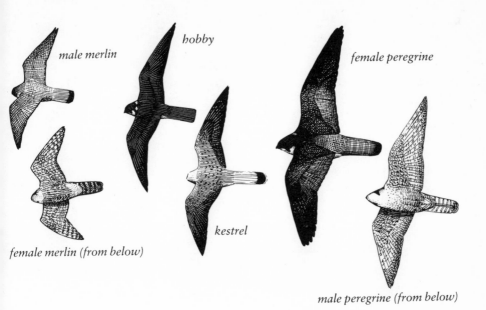

*male merlin*

*hobby*

*female peregrine*

*female merlin (from below)*

*kestrel*

*male peregrine (from below)*

peregrine (33-4 cm/13-14 in for both sexes), the hobby is also an aerial predator but with less sexual dimorphism in size. They seem very swift-like in flight, with long, narrow wings and a short tail. The adults are again slate-grey above and white underneath, but the undersides are streaked, not barred, and the thighs and under-tail are a beautiful chestnut colour. The moustache is slightly narrower than in peregrines, but still stands out in adults. The juveniles are dark brown above, heavily streaked below and lack those wonderful orange trousers.

Peregrines and hobbies are more typical of other falcons in having identical plumage for both sexes. The blue-grey colour and sharp contrast between upper and lower plumage is also typical of bird-eating raptors, and may make them less conspicuous when attacking prey. The differing plumage of the sexes in the other two species is more difficult to understand. Merlins often nest on the ground and kestrels occasionally do, so a less conspicuous plumage may help to hide females from predators. This might also apply to the juvenile plumage of all four species, which develops while the young are in the nest and is drab and brown.

Falcon Facts 1: **Size and appearance**

|  | Peregrine | Merlin | Kestrel | Hobby |
|---|---|---|---|---|
| **Male** | | | | |
| Weight | 680 g (1.50 lb) | 162 g (0.36 lb) | 197 g (0.43 lb) | 182 g (0.40 lb) |
| Wing length | 309 mm (12.2 in) | 199 mm (7.8 in) | 246 mm (9.7 in) | 256 mm (10.1 in) |
| Colour | slate-grey | blue-grey | red-brown | slate-grey |
| **Female** | | | | |
| Weight | 1,125 g (2.48 lb) | 212 g (0.47 lb) | 254 g (0.56 lb) | 241 g (0.53 lb) |
| Wing length | 365 mm (14.4 in) | 217 mm (8.5 in) | 256 mm (10.1 in) | 268 mm (10.6 in) |
| Colour | slate-grey | dark-brown | brown | slate-grey |
| **Dimorphism:** How much bigger is the female than the male? | 15% | 9% | 4% | 5% |

# Distribution and habitat

All four species of falcon in Britain have a wide geographical distribution. This is a result of their strong powers of flight, which enable them to disperse over long distances, and their ability to breed in a variety of open-country habitats. The British countryside has been profoundly altered (some would say vandalized) by humans for many centuries. We have cleared forest to make grassland for our stock and room for crops, and drained and cultivated wetlands. So, apart from the highest Scottish mountains, falcons are living in a man-made environment from which they have both benefited and suffered. The benefits resulted from the clearing of forest, which probably led to an increase in the abundance of open-country falcons at the expense of forest-dwelling raptors such as goshawks. The detrimental effects of human activity are more recent and diverse, but include the loss of habitat to intensive farming, the loss of breeding sites through disturbance and the poisoning of the food supply by the use of pesticides. To some extent, then, the distributions of falcons depend on their ability to thrive in the conditions we provide for them.

In general, summer distribution reflects the availability of food and nesting sites, while winter distribution depends on how climate affects the abundance and availability of food. Few small birds are adapted to living in prolonged snow-cover, and many of the species eaten by peregrines and merlins move to low ground in winter. Rodents can survive well under thick snow, but snow protects them from kestrels, which therefore tend to seek milder climates. Hobbies feed on large flying insects, or insectivorous birds, so they are unable to cope with cold winters and are entirely migratory in Europe.

**Peregrines.** There are few parts of the world that do not have peregrines either breeding, wintering or permanently resident. Breeding populations occur from the high Arctic, through the tropics to the tip of South America and Tasmania. The few habitats that defeat them include extreme deserts, permanent ice-caps, open steppes and dense forest. Birds breeding in the Arctic migrate long distances: North American birds to South and Central America; Scandinavian and Siberian ones to central Europe or Asia.

Despite this worldwide distribution, peregrines in Britain are confined largely to the north and west. This reflects the distribution of their cliff nesting-sites along rocky western coasts and in uplands. Traditional coastal sites occur at suitable cliffs from Kent westwards to Land's End and northwards to Durness. The east coastal sites are mainly in Scotland or in North Yorkshire. Inland strongholds are the Highlands and Southern Uplands of Scotland, the Lake District and Pennines in England and the Welsh Mountains. In winter, peregrines try to stay near these breeding sites if they can, but move to nearby low ground and shorelines to find food when snow is thick in the hills. The strong association of peregrines with wild and desolate areas of mountain and moorland, or towering sea cliffs, adds to their aura as symbols of fierce independence and intractability.

**Merlins** are birds of open spaces with scattered trees and low ground-cover. They are northerners, breeding in Europe, Siberia and North America. Although they are found further north than other small falcons (breeding up to 71°N), they cannot survive in winter where the mean temperature is below freezing, so populations in much of Scandinavia, Siberia and Arctic North America are totally migratory. North American merlins winter in the southern USA and Central America, while north European birds migrate to Central Europe and even into North Africa.

In Britain, merlins tend to breed in peregrine country, though they don't seem to like coastal areas and confine themselves more to the uplands. Their greater choice of nesting sites makes them more widely distributed in the uplands than peregrines, though they seem unable to breed in the low ground they occupy in winter. Few low-ground areas have breeding pairs now, the traditional sites such as bogs and mosses in Cumbria and coastal dunes in south Wales and south-west England being largely abandoned. Merlins that breed in uplands tend to move to low ground and coasts in winter, resulting in a movement to the south-east.

*Merlin over young plantation.*

**Kestrels.** Few people would be surprised to find that kestrels are our most widespread raptor, with breeding records from virtually the whole country. Kestrels have the widest range of both prey and nesting sites of any falcon, and this allows them to exploit moorlands, farmland and even large cities. Their strongholds are probably the uplands of northern England and southern Scotland where there are large tracts of rough grassland suited to voles and other mammal prey.

Kestrels of one sort or another are found across the world, and our species is found throughout Europe, much of Asia and right down to South Africa. Very similar species breed in the East Indies and Australia, so kestrels cover most of the Old World. The New World has its own species, the American kestrel, which can be seen hovering from Hudson's Bay to the Tierra del Fuego. Unlike cars and hamburgers, the American variety of kestrel is *smaller* than ours.

Northern populations that breed in areas of permanent winter snow-cover migrate: in Europe as far as north and West Africa, in America as far as Central and South America. British kestrels are partially migrant in the north, with some individuals braving it out in winter but many moving into central and southern England or onto the Continent. Southern

# City slickers

Several species of falcon regularly nest in towns and cities. Kestrels are renowned for their urban lifestyle, and can be found in cities throughout the world. Peregrines, too, will often find a home amid the traffic and noise, especially if there is a good supply of pigeons at hand. Peregrines have been released in many North American cities and seem to readily swap towering cliffs for towering skyscrapers. British peregrines have, alas, not caught the city habit to the same extent, but there is no reason why they too might not become urbanized.

Merlins are not birds you normally associate with towns or cities. But some in the Canadian prairies of Saskatchewan and Alberta have moved into the suburbs and centres of cities such as Calgary, Edmonton and Saskatoon. Trees are scarce on the prairies, but were widely planted around human settlements. When these trees matured they provided nest sites for crows and magpies, which spread across the plains from town to town. In the early 1970s it was noticed that a few merlin pairs had begun to nest in some of the old crow's nests. The population in Saskatoon has been monitored closely by Lynn Oliphant and his co-workers. After a slow start, the number of breeding pairs expanded rapidly and the city now boasts over 30 pairs. Colonization was given a helping hand in Regina, where 6 merlins were deliberately released in 1979. They soon began breeding, and the population is now well established.

City merlins feed on the abundant house sparrows, and this has ensured excellent breeding success and created some unusually high densities. In 1982, the 16 pairs in Saskatoon were in an area of only 29 $km^2$ (11 sq miles), with pairs a mere 1-2 km (0.6-1.2 miles) apart. Such dense populations cannot be fully supported by the food available in the city, and some males fly to outlying farmsteads to find food. The shelter and year-round food supply has encouraged some merlins to remain on breeding territories over winter, unlike their

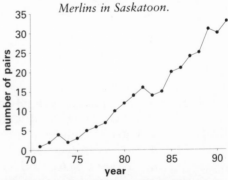

Merlins in Saskatoon.

The growth of the merlin population in Saskatoon followed by a pattern typical of new colonization — a slow start followed by rapid increase which gradually declined as the habitat filled to capacity.

rural forebears who migrate to warmer climes.

The Canadian merlins have proved remarkably adaptable and successful. Those breeding in cities no longer begin calling every time someone approaches the nest tree, and many people are unaware that they have merlins breeding in their gardens! Towns in Britain have plenty of sparrows and nesting crows, so maybe one day we will be able to boast our own Falco columbarius urbanii.

Streetwise Merlins

populations tend to be largely sedentary, and remain on their breeding grounds throughout the year.

**Hobbies** breed across much of Europe, Siberia and in parts of Asia. However, they require warm, dry conditions that encourage large insects to fly, so they avoid countries with a moist, oceanic climate. Britain is therefore on the north-western edge of their range, and here they are largely birds of south-east and central England. Most bird-watchers imagine hobbies breeding in small clumps of Scot's pine on the heaths and downland of Hampshire, Surrey or Sussex. These are certainly its strongholds, but it is by no means restricted to these areas, and substantial numbers breed in the Midland counties and East Anglia. Hobbies become rather secretive during the incubation period, and are easily missed when breeding, so their distribution in England has probably been underestimated. Nonetheless, they are scarce in northern England and there are only scattered records from Scotland and Wales.

Unlike the other three species, hobbies are totally migratory in Europe, though there are odd records of birds found in winter on the Continent and I have seen them in the East Midlands in late November. The wintering areas are in Africa south of the equator, where the warm climate and seasonal rains produce swarms of termites and other large insects. These are the main winter food for hobbies and other migrant falcons such as lesser kestrels and red-footed falcons.

The distribution of the British falcon highlights both the similarities and differences in their lifestyles. Peregrines and merlins both feed on open-country birds and are mainly uplanders, though peregrines can additionally exploit the cliffs and seabirds at coastal sites. Hobbies rarely mingle with these two species, being confined to warmer, lower areas and able to exploit the more tree-filled habitats of southern England. Kestrels overlap with all three species and are the least specialized in their requirements. They take more mammals than birds or insects, and may therefore be able to co-exist with bird-eating falcons without directly competing for food.

# Studying falcons

Some bird-watchers are not content with just watching birds. Scientists in particular are inquisitive creatures, prone to asking awkward questions from an early age. They are also highly suspicious. If you tell them you see the same kestrel every day sitting on the same telephone pole on your way to work, a scientist will want to know if it really *is* the same bird. And a host of other questions: how long does it live? What size is its territory? Does it breed in the same place year after year? Where does it go to in the winter? To answer these questions you have to mark birds so that you can tell them apart.

The standard method of individually marking birds is to use a numbered metal leg-ring. Each number is unique, and the ring carries an address to which anyone can send details of where and when the bird was found. Records of birds found dead or injured are called 'recoveries', and give valuable information about movements and mortality. British rings have the address of the national museum, but this is just a holding address for the British Trust for Ornithology (BTO) who administer ringing in this country. Rings are the best way to mark a large number of individuals, and are used whatever other methods might be needed as well.

Falconers have been marking some of their prized birds with silver rings or chains for centuries, but the first attempts to ring wild birds began within the last eighty years or so. The early pioneers ran their own schemes, such as that started by H. F. Witherby in 1907 and publicized through the magazine *British Birds*. As ringing became more popular it had to be centralized and carefully regulated, and the BTO took on this role in 1937. There has been a rapid growth in ringing in recent decades, and considerable numbers of falcons are ringed each year.

The problem with numbered rings is that you can only identify your

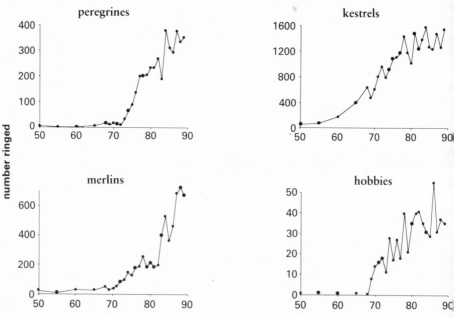

*Interest in falcons has grown rapidly since the 1960s, and this is reflected in the numbers ringed each year. In the case of peregrines and hobbies, the increase may also reflect the increasing populations over this period. Kestrels make up the majority of ringed falcons in Britain; the rapid increase of the 1970s has levelled off now, and the 3-4 year cycles in the number ringed may reflect changes in density and breeding success due to cycles in vole numbers.*

bird if you trap it or find it dead, rather than if you see it flying. Biologists need a way to identify birds on sight. One solution is to use coloured rings, and this works well for some species that can carry several rings because different colour sequences on each leg can then be used to mark uniquely dozens of individuals. Falcons, however, have relatively short legs, and can rarely be approached closely enough to identify the colours. A better method is to attach small plastic tags to the wings. This can be done using steel or nylon pins that are pushed through the thin flap of skin at the front of the wing. The process is quick and painless, though handling falcons during such an operation requires practice to prevent them lacerating your fingers!

By choosing tags of different colours, or with large numbers on, it is possible to individually mark dozens of birds, and the tags usually stay on for life. The birds treat them as feathers, particularly if the tags are made of soft nylon cloth (the kind of material used for lorry tarpaulins). I wing-tagged hundreds of full-grown birds during my fourteen years of studying kestrels. A few tore their tags off, but most kept them on, some for over six years.

Wing-tagging gives valuable information on how long birds stay on their territories, how widely they range and how often they change their nesting sites. It is particularly useful for birds like kestrels that are easily seen and tend to have fairly small ranges. Other species are less obliging and a more sophisticated approach is needed to measure their territory size or follow their movements. Radio-tags have been used for many years to track wild animals. At first they were cumbersome packages that could only be used on elephants or moose! Gradually the technology improved

Prototype radio tags were somewhat cumbersome

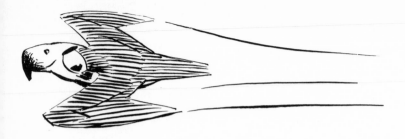

and a whole new world of study opened to ornithologists when batteries and circuits became small enough to fit onto birds.

The transmitter weighs a few grams and is attached either by a body-harness or to the base of the tail feathers. It emits a signal at a fixed frequency that continues for anything up to a year, depending on the size of the transmitter. With luck, the 4 g transmitters I used on kestrels lasted 4-6 months. They have a range of several miles, provided there are no obstacles between the transmitter and receiver. The latter is usually a hand-held device that looks a bit like a lunch box attached to a television aerial. Point the aerial at the bird and you get the loudest signal. Radio

## Playing tag

*Finding the right way of attaching tags can be a frustrating business, and peregrines in particular have proved tricky customers. Scientists in Idaho made several attempts at looping tags over the wing without attaching them by pins. They released birds in eager anticipation, but were soon cursing as they watched the peregrines tear the tags off at the first opportunity. The same thing happened to a falconer who wanted to radio-track peregrines on migration. At first he tried a harness, but that lasted only two days. Tying to the tail was even less successful until he used the falconer's trick of 'imping' it to the tail feathers. The vane of the feather has no nerves and is quite strong, so falconers replace broken feathers by sewing shed feathers to the base of the old one. This works well with transmitters, which can be sewn into the base of the tail feathers so that the short wire antenna lies down the feather vane. The transmitter falls off when the feathers are lost in the annual moult and can often be recovered and used again with a new battery.*

transmitters allow you to find your bird quickly and follow it continuously. However, they are much more expensive than wing tags and are not permanent markers.

*Wing tag on a kestrel.*

## Big brother is watching

The biologist or falconer tracking his bird can attract the curiosity of passers-by, and sometimes cause a certain amount of panic. When I began tracking kestrels in a remote part of Scotland, the sight of a stranger wearing earphones and waving an antenna around caused a rush of applications for television licences at the local post office! On another occasion I was tracking a bird that flew across an air-force base, and it took me some time to convince the military police that I was not spying.

# The fall and rise of Reginald Peregrine: the pesticide story

Peregrines have been the star players in an environmental drama that unfolded in the early 1960s, long before anyone had heard of 'green' politics. The villains of the piece were a group of chemicals called organochlorines (or OCs for short), of which DDT is the most well known (or to give it its full, snappy title: dichloro-diphenyl-trichloroethane!). DDT is a good guy turned bad: in 1939 it was found to be a potent insecticide, and was usefully employed during the war to kill harmful insects such as malaria mosquitoes, ticks and locusts. Being relatively harmless to humans but extremely long-lasting, it could be sprayed anywhere and one application would give protection for months. It was only later that its harmful effects on wildlife became apparent, and by then it had been joined by 'cyclodiene' compounds, such as aldrin and dieldrin, which were also OCs, but more poisonous than DDT.

Peregrines feature in the story for several reasons. Although many birds and mammals accumulate OCs, predators are often the most seriously affected because they are near the top of food chains. As persistent pollutants such as OCs pass from plants to animals and from prey to predator they become concentrated in tissues and are more likely to cause

*Adult peregrine.*

problems. Bird-eating raptors such as peregrines, merlins and sparrowhawks are at the end of longer food chains than are mammal-eaters such as kestrels or owls, so they tend to accumulate more pesticides. Even at doses too weak to kill, these chemicals can disrupt breeding by damaging a bird's physiology or behaviour. Any decline in population density was more likely to be noticed in peregrines than in other species because peregrines nest on traditional sites that are well known to bird-watchers and egg-collectors. Some cliffs have been visited each year for decades, so it was possible to collate records and obtain a reasonable estimate of peregrine breeding numbers both before and after OCs were in use. Furthermore, many of the early visitors were egg collectors and their spoils, still intact in museums and private collections, were to provide vital evidence of the timing and extent of the problem.

The story began in the 1950s with scattered evidence that all was not well with British peregrines. There was a sudden decline in Cornwall after 1955 and Derek Ratcliffe, a life-long devotee of the species, began to find broken eggshells at eyries (nests) he visited. Ironically, it was a complaint from pigeon fanciers that peregrines were too numerous that sparked an enquiry into their status in Britain in 1961. Systematic checks were made of known breeding sites, and it was soon clear that something was drastically wrong. A mere 68 per cent of sites used before the war were now occupied, and this dropped to 44 per cent in the next two years. Even where territories were occupied, many pairs failed to lay or broke their eggs so that the production of young was unnaturally low.

The extent of the decline was not uniform across the country. Peregrines in England and Wales were more seriously affected than those in Scotland, and coastal sites everywhere were heavily depleted. The least affected areas were the south and east Highlands of Scotland, where breeding numbers were virtually unchanged. The decline in Britain was repeated across much of Europe, and in North America peregrines became extinct everywhere east of the Rocky Mountains. The drama, it seemed, was being played on an international stage.

At first the cause of the decline remained a mystery. However, chemical analyses of addled peregrine eggs and tissues from the increasing number of dead individuals being found showed that they contained traces of DDE (the form that DDT takes in animal tissues) and HEOD (the active ingredient of aldrin and dieldrin). Both these chemicals were by then being widely used in agriculture, and dieldrin was known to have caused the deaths of many small birds and raptors in East Anglia when it was used as a seed dressing for spring-sown cereals. DDT, though not directly killing birds, was found to interfere with one of the enzymes involved in producing the eggshell, resulting in eggs with thin shells. These eggs were easily broken by the incubating female and, even if they remained intact, the embryo was likely to die. The areas where numbers declined most severely were those nearest to arable farmland, such as coastal sites of England, Wales and east Scotland. It seemed likely that peregrines were eating contaminated prey that passed through their breeding grounds, or were catching such prey on low ground in winter.

Derek Ratcliffe added to the evidence by working out how to measure the relative thickness of eggshells. Dividing the weight of the empty shell by the size of the egg (length × breadth) gave an index of shell thinning without having to destroy the egg. This was important because it allowed him to sample eggs taken over many years by collectors and thus establish the timing and extent of shell thinning. Thin shells first appeared in 1947, the year after pigeon fanciers first began dusting their birds with DDT to kill feather lice. The average thickness of shells, unchanged for at least a hundred years, suddenly slumped by 20 per cent. This early and direct route of contamination was later confirmed when pigeon leg-rings, meticulously collected and labelled from a site in 1947, were found to be covered in minute traces of DDT.

So careful detective work by ornithologists and chemists had shown that peregrines suffered a double blow from organochlorines. From 1947, DDT had reduced breeding output by thinning eggshells. Then, after 1955, cyclodienes caused widespread declines in peregrine breeding numbers by killing full-grown birds that ate contaminated prey. Of the two chemicals, dieldrin was probably most important in reducing populations because lowered breeding success alone could not have caused such a rapid decline. Under normal conditions, about 90 per cent of breeding peregrines survive from one year to the next, so it would take about eight years for the population to decline to 44 per cent of its original level, even if *no* young were fledged anywhere. In some areas of England and Wales the populations were virtually wiped out in less than five years, which must have been due to increased adult mortality as well as to poorer breeding. Reduced breeding output from DDT may have speeded the decline, but it was the combined effects of the OCs that wrought so much damage in British peregrines.

Because of the mounting evidence, the use of OCs was gradually curtailed from 1962, first by voluntary restrictions and finally by legally enforced bans in the 1980s. Cyclodienes such as dieldrin were withdrawn from spring cereal use in 1962 and from autumn cereals in 1975. DDT was progressively restricted over the same period, but was still heavily used in fruit-growing areas until the 1980s. This, together with its extreme persistence in the environment, made it slower to decline in peregrine eggs than cyclodienes. Peregrines began to recover as the restrictions came into force and levels of OCs in eggs and tissues declined. Eggshells began to get thicker, and breeding performance improved in most areas. By 1971 overall numbers were back to 54 per cent of pre-war levels, though recovery was very uneven with many coastal sites showing no sign of reoccupation. The slower recovery along coasts was associated with higher contamination with OCs and mercury (another harmful pollutant), possibly because prey such as waders and seabirds were accumulating high levels from polluted estuaries. A repeated survey in 1981 showed that numbers were virtually back to normal in much of Scotland and northern England, and things were improving further south and along some coastlines. This was the last detailed survey, and the estimate for the total United Kingdom population was 768 pairs. Since then, numbers have continued to increase and in several districts are now higher than they were before pesticides struck. This might be because of reduced persecution from egg-collectors and gamekeepers compared with the pre-war years. The total population in 1991 could be approaching 1,000 pairs.

In Britain, peregrines came back fairly quickly with very little help from humans (apart from rectifying the initial blunder). Some populations went relatively unscathed, especially those in the Scottish Highlands that fed mainly on uncontaminated grouse. The young that were fledged when the population was low were able to rapidly recolonize former sites when the levels of dieldrin declined and survival improved. In the USA, however, peregrines were eliminated from such huge areas that recolonization would have been very slow indeed. Fortunately, humans took a positive role in the saga this time, by rearing peregrines in captivity and releasing them into the wild. Charities such as the Peregrine Fund have made a major contribution to restoring wild populations and along the way have contributed a great deal to our knowledge of peregrine breeding behaviour. Perhaps, after all, this cloud has a silver lining.

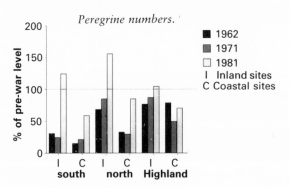

*Peregrine numbers.*

*Peregrines were surveyed throughout Britain at ten-year intervals, and numbers expressed as a percentage of the pre-war population. In 1962, the declines were worst in southern England and Wales ('south') and in coastal areas of northern England and south Scotland ('north'), while the Highlands of Scotland were relatively unscathed. The marked recovery since 1971 has mainly been at inland sites, where some populations are now higher than before the war.*

# Giving peregrines a helping hand

The use of captive breeding programmes for endangered species has become an important conservation technique over the last thirty years, applied to species as diverse as Californian condors, bald eagles and Mauritius kestrels. The peregrine was the first species to be successfully helped in this way, pioneering methods that are now commonplace. The experience of falconers was vital in creating the early breeding centres, which had to experiment with various aviaries and breeding regimes before rearing chicks became routine. Scientific research went hand in

# Natural selection in action

The peregrines that disappeared from the eastern United States were a particular race with a distinctive colouring. Many animal species vary in size and coloration in different parts of their range. Scientists call the different forms 'races' or 'sub-species', though the variations may be slight and there is often disagreement as to whether or not a particular population is a distinct race. The racial variation across the peregrine's huge geographic range probably reflects the isolation of widely separated populations. Individuals from, say, Alaska are very unlikely to meet or breed with those from Europe, so over time the two populations acquire a slightly different cross-section of genes. The question facing the scientists that wanted to re-introduce peregrines to the eastern states was whether these racial differences are in some way adaptive: was the appearance of the eastern peregrines just a chance variation, or the result of generations of selection for genes that increased survival in that particular region? Certainly some of the racial features of peregrines are likely to have evolved for good reasons because they reflect trends seen in many other species. For example, races nearer the poles tend to be larger than those nearer the equator, which may help birds in colder climates to conserve heat.

Rather than breed from one particular race, the researchers decided to use a variety of parents, to ensure a wide genetic base for the re-introduced population. Nature could then take its course, and individuals should be selected that were best adapted to that particular habitat. It will be interesting to see if the resulting race is similar to those that lived there originally, but you and I may not be around to test the hypothesis!

hand with the captive programme, and tricks such as artificial insemination and double clutching were used to improve output. Double clutching means removing eggs from females soon after they are laid and hatching them in an incubator. The female will usually lay another clutch, which she is allowed to rear herself. In this way, twice as many chicks can be reared from a given number of birds.

There are several ways of returning chicks to the wild. In the Rocky Mountains some wild breeding pairs remained but they hatched only a few chicks and the population could not sustain itself. Captive-bred young were added to these nests, and the fostered chicks successfully reared by wild parents. Where the population is extinct, young birds must be gradually introduced to the wild, a process called 'hacking' by falconers. Well grown chicks are moved to a large box on a cliff or tower. The boxes have bars at the front to allow the birds to view their surroundings and recognize them as 'home'. The birds are fed daily, sometimes through a long pipe led into the box from higher up the cliff. This makes feeding less hazardous and ensures the young birds have minimum contact with their keepers. If young falcons learn to associate food with humans, they can begin to behave as if they have human parents: screaming and begging every time a human comes into view. Later in life, such 'imprinted' birds may try to mate with their human keepers, and such abnormal behaviour obviously renders them useless for release into the wild.

The box is opened when the chicks are ready to fly, at about 45 days old. They are fed near the box on a 'hack board', which they soon learn to associate with food. At first they rely entirely on this food, but then gradually disperse from the site as they learn to hunt for themselves.

Over 3,000 peregrines have been introduced to the wild in the USA since 1974. The first few years were depressingly slow, and in the east it took 5 years and several hundred releases before the first pair bred in the wild in 1979. The reasons for the delay are not known, but it was not simply a case of waiting for birds to mature physically because peregrines can breed when a year old. The survival rate of hacked birds may not be as good as wild reared ones, possibly because they do not have the benefit of learning from their parents. But population growth can be rapid once released birds begin breeding successfully, and the population in the eastern United States grew from 3 to 40 pairs in just 7 years.

# Merlin magic: a disappearing act?

Merlins, like peregrines, are bird-eaters, so they are also vulnerable to pesticides. But whereas peregrines have made a successful recovery, merlins have not. It is widely believed that merlins have been declining in Britain since the turn of the century, though there is scant information about their pre-war status so it is difficult to be certain. Losses due to pesticides may have hastened the decline, as may changes in land use in the uplands. Concern over the status of merlins has prompted several population studies around the country (notably in Northumberland, Wales, north-east Scotland, Orkney and Shetland), and a national survey in 1983-4. The latter confirmed the declining numbers, and estimated there to be about 500-700 pairs across Britain. The local studies suggest that the extent of the decline may vary from place to place and can be caused by several factors:

**Pesticides.** Information about merlin numbers from the pesticide era is very scant. Ian Newton, who has helped to co-ordinate several merlin studies, gleaned some historical records of merlin sites in the Peak District,

*Ground-nesting merlins are vulnerable to foxes.*

many of which were first abandoned during the 1950s and 1960s. Merlins carry higher levels of pesticides than any other British raptor, and numbers are likely to have suffered as a result. Their heavy contamination may stem from their small size because, pound for pound, they have to eat more food than larger raptors and therefore ingest more pollutants.

But why haven't merlins recovered as these pollutants have been withdrawn from use? The levels of DDT and dieldrin in merlin eggs have declined significantly since the 1960s, and so are probably not a major factor reducing breeding success in most populations. This is not to say that merlins are entirely untroubled: a recent survey has shown that poor breeding success in some pairs is associated with high levels of mercury in eggs. Mercury is used as a seed-dressing and has been implicated in declines in raptor numbers in other countries. However, it also seems to be naturally abundant in some areas such as Orkney and Shetland, where all merlin eggs have high mercury levels but breeding is no worse than on the mainland.

**Habitat change.** One reason frequently suggested for the merlin's demise is a long-term decline in suitable breeding habitat. British merlins are associated with heather moorland that is managed for grouse shooting. This habitat has come under pressure from afforestation, increased sheep numbers and the improvement of grassland in the uplands. Such changes might affect merlins in two ways: by reducing the number of small birds (and hence merlin food), or by destroying nesting habitat. Colin Bibby's detailed study of merlins in Wales showed that they prefer to nest in areas of extensive heather moorland and this is where breeding is most successful. But whether this is because they suffer fewer losses, or because they have more food is not known. His results differed from those in other areas such as Northumberland, where pairs nesting on the ground in heather were less successful than those nesting in trees in grassland. The declines in many areas are not obviously related to a loss of habitat, and there often seem to be sufficient places for merlins to nest, but not enough merlins to occupy them.

**Breeding success.** The apparent shortage of merlins to occupy sites suggests that numbers may decline because breeding productivity is too low to sustain the population. In several studies, population declines were associated with poor breeding success, but we do not know enough about merlin populations to tell if this could lead to a shortage of breeders. The reasons for poor breeding success seem to vary from place to place and even from year to year in the same place. Most losses in Northumberland were due to predation of the young, especially those in ground nests. In

*Female merlin.*                    *Adult male kestrel.*

Orkney, most pairs failed during incubation and there were frequent signs of broken eggs. Merlins are vulnerable to cold, wet springs because rain soaks nests and makes small birds hard to catch. The better summers of 1989 and 1990 improved breeding success, only to have it washed away in the rains of 1991!

**Human disturbance.** The effects of humans on nesting merlins are hard to quantify, but they are rarely beneficial. Well meaning hill-walkers may inadvertently disturb sites that are near to footpaths, but this is unlikely to be a widespread problem. More deliberate interference is possible from those who take eggs, or young chicks for falconry, or from gamekeepers trying to protect their grouse chicks. Nest robbing has increased in some areas, and may be locally damaging to well known sites. However, this does not mean that the site will be abandoned, and there are some cases where merlins have returned year after year to sites that have never fledged any chicks. Disturbance by gamekeeping is rare, and keepers may actually help merlins by killing predators such as stoats and foxes or by maintaining the high quality of heather moors.

The picture for merlins is thus rather confused and in need of careful monitoring. Despite the gloom and uncertainty, there are some encouraging signs. Merlins in Northumberland and Wales were recently found nesting in old crow's-nests in large blocks of forestry plantation. No one knows for certain how long this has been happening because nests are so hard to find, and it may have made the decline look worse than it really was if pairs abandoned traditional sites to sneak off unnoticed into the forest. In several other areas the declines of the early 1980s seem to have been halted or reversed, and numbers are slowly rising again. The growing number of population studies may eventually help to unravel the complex causes of the merlin's decline and so present a long-term solution.

# Kestrels, kestrels everywhere . . .

Kestrels feed mainly on small mammals, which have lower pesticide levels than small birds. Although kestrels were affected by organochlorine pesticides, their decline was less widespread or severe than in peregrines or merlins. The areas of most intense pesticide use were south-east England, particularly the Cambridgeshire fens. Kestrels became rare breeding birds in these areas for much of the 1960s and 1970s, but numbers had largely recovered by the time I began studying them in the fens in 1981. The *Atlas of Breeding Birds*, produced by the BTO in 1976, showed kestrels bred in nearly all the 10 × 10 km grid-squares in Britain and Ireland. They were absent only from Shetland and some parts of East Anglia. A similar survey in 1988-91 showed increases in south-east England, but an apparent decline in parts of the West and in Ireland. It is not certain if this decline is real and, if so, what has caused it. Estimating the total UK population from such surveys is extremely difficult because the density in each grid square may vary three- or four-fold. Taking an average of 20 pairs per 100 square kilometres, the total population would be about 60,000 pairs.

Although kestrels are widely distributed in Britain, they are not equally abundant in all areas. Kestrels occur at their highest densities where there is plenty of rough grassland that is suitable for voles. Some of the best kestrel habitats are the young conifer plantations created in the uplands since the war. There is a rapid growth of grass after planting because sheep and deer are excluded, and this provides ideal habitat for voles. For about ten years the plantations bulge with kestrels and other vole-eating predators such as long- and short-eared owls, foxes and weasels. During this stage, the density of kestrels may reach 30-40 pairs/100 km$^2$ (0.8-1.0 pairs/sq mile). The growing trees eventually smother the ground vegetation as the plantation enters the thicket stage. Voles become confined to small rides and the kestrels and owls are replaced by sparrowhawks who feed on the now numerous songbirds.

Kestrels are usually less abundant where they have to rely on prey other than voles. Densities in lowland farms in England are about 15-25 pairs/ 100 km$^2$ in mixed arable-livestock areas and as low as 10 pairs/100 km$^2$ in the intensive arable farmland of the Cambridgeshire fens. This means that kestrels are three or four times more abundant in the best vole habitats than in the worst. On the other hand some urban areas with little vole habitat have high kestrel densities because of the abundance of sparrows and other bird prey.

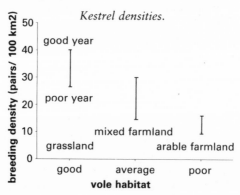

*In any given habitat, kestrel numbers vary from year to year but are generally higher where there is plenty of rough grassland suitable for voles.*

Biologists have known for many years that voles and lemmings vary in abundance from year to year. In northern Europe these changes occur in a regular cycle, with high numbers about every 3-4 years. The further north you go the more regular the cycles, and the greater the difference in density between peak and trough years. In northern Scandinavia there are occasional 'plague' years, where voles can be seen everywhere and it is difficult to walk through grass without stepping on them. Kestrels and other vole predators are adapted to take advantage of these bountiful conditions, and breed at high densities, and rear large broods, during good vole years. For example, in one Finnish study area there were 37 pairs during a vole plague but only 6 pairs when vole numbers crashed.

There are many theories about what causes these vole cycles, but this still remains a mystery. Predators are unlikely to make voles decline because they take only a fraction of the vole population during peak years. However, they may alter the timing of the cycles by keeping numbers in check during low years. Kestrels in these northern areas are largely migratory, and the population can build up rapidly in spring as migrants settle where food is abundant. There is no time-lag between any increase in vole numbers and a corresponding increase in kestrels. Less mobile predators, such as stoats or foxes, have to breed in order to increase local densities, so their numbers tend to lag behind that of the voles.

The critical factors controlling kestrel breeding densities vary from place to place. In northern areas, many kestrels migrate away in autumn, so the severity of the local winter weather is unlikely to affect numbers in spring. However, the open areas of upland and tundra have few nesting places for kestrels, and some of the birds that arrive in spring are unable to find a place to breed, even though they have ample food. In southern lowlands kestrels are mainly sedentary, so spring numbers may be affected by the winter vole density or weather. If voles are scarce, or there is prolonged snow, many residents will die and density will be low in spring. Furthermore, these lowland areas are now intensively farmed, leaving little vole habitat. Spring food supply is often poor and many birds are unable to breed even though there are plenty of suitable nesting sites.

# Hidden hobbies

We know less about the numbers of hobbies in Britain than any of the other three falcons. Hobbies rarely breed at high densities so their nests are widely scattered. Anyone wanting to study hobbies must cover a lot of

*Adult hobby.*

ground, with all the problems of getting access, high travel costs and finding time to search large tracts of countryside. The birds don't help much because they arrive late in the season and are quiet around the nest during incubation, making it difficult to find pairs even though they nest in the same territories from year to year.

Despite these difficulties, the few studies of hobbies in Britain indicate they are on the up and up. Hobbies have considerably expanded their range in England over the last twenty years and now breed as far north as Yorkshire. Recent surveys for the new breeding atlas have found substantial numbers north of the Wash-Severn line, where formerly there were few pairs. Estimates of the total population vary from about 500 to 850 pairs. Although some of the increase may be due to more thorough searching, it is unlikely that the newly colonized areas were traditional strongholds because egg-collectors do not mention many sites there, and they rarely missed them. The present increase thus seems to be a genuine expansion of range, and not simply a recovery to a pre-pesticide status, an idea confirmed by the generally low levels of pesticides in hobby eggs (usually higher than in kestrels but lower than peregrines). Whether it is due to reduced persecution, a warming climate or changes in the African wintering grounds is unclear.

Some idea of the increase can be gained from the records submitted to the rare breeding birds panel since 1977, though such records are the tip of the iceberg rather than accurate estimates of the total British population. Based on the number of grid squares occupied, the total population is likely to be at least 850 pairs, considerably more than the 60-90 estimated for the 1950s.

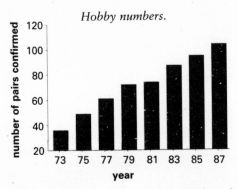

*Hobby numbers.*

*The number of breeding hobbies reported to the rare breeding birds panel has increased steadily over the last twenty years, reflecting the increased distribution of the species in England.*

Nesting densities in Britain have been measured in two studies in the 1980s, one in southern England and the other in the south Midlands. In southern England, hobbies were most abundant in the New Forest, with about 5 pairs/100 km$^2$. Densities in farmland were about 2 pairs/100 km$^2$ and less than this on downland. In the Midlands, densities seem to range from 3-5 pairs/100 km$^2$, not very different from the more southern areas that were the traditional strongholds.

One of the longest studies of hobbies has been in Berlin, where hobbies used to nest at high densities in the city's large heaths and woodland. In the 1960s there were some 27 pairs in 67 km$^2$ (26 sq miles) of woodland, but this density (40 pairs/100 km$^2$) is almost certainly inflated because it

*Hobby over heathland.*

did not include urban areas where there were no hobbies. Whatever the true figure, it has declined since then, with fewer than 10 pairs in the same area in the 1980s. The cause of this dramatic decline is not known, but breeding success has not declined over the same period. The fact that hobby numbers can simultaneously go up in Britain and down in Berlin without an adequate explanation in either case is a slight embarrassment to professional falconologists. Elusive birds, hobbies . . .

The Hobby is indeed a shy thing

# Food

Finding out what a raptor eats is an important step towards understanding its ecology, and there have been numerous studies on the diet of falcons in Britain. Two striking facts emerge from these studies: first, that if you sample for long enough you will discover your species eats almost *anything*; second, that individuals usually concentrate on a comparatively limited range of prey. What these apparently contradictory facts suggest is that falcons are physically capable of killing most animals up to a certain size and recognize a wide variety as potential food. From this potentially wide range they select certain species, probably because how and where the falcon chooses to hunt favours some prey species over others, and these form the bulk of the diet.

'YOUR BIRD WILL EAT ANYTHING'

**Measuring falcon diets.** Finding out what falcons eat requires a great deal of patience, a Sherlock Holmes mentality and a keen eye for detail. Like all raptors, falcons regurgitate pellets of undigested food remains at roosts or nests. Examining these pellets can give useful clues to what the falcon has been eating, but only if they have ingested reasonable quantities of fur, bones or feathers. Pellet analysis is particularly useful for kestrels, which eat mammal prey and produce relatively large pellets. The bird-eaters pluck most of the feathers from their kills and the small pellets they produce are of little use for identifying prey species. However, this can be done by collecting the plucked feathers found in and around the nest during the breeding season. A trained eye can identify even obscure species from a single feather, and thus build up a picture of which species are taken and how frequently.

Obviously there are errors in these methods due to the differing digestibility of prey or visibility of feathers. Earthworms leave far fewer remains in pellets than do voles, and a pile of white pigeon feathers is easier to find than the remains of a skylark. But, for better or worse, these are the only practical ways of measuring the diets of many different individuals. Used carefully, they can show how the diet varies between species, over time or in different habitats.

# The beginners' guide to pellet analysis

Female kestrel.

*Kestrel pellets are easier to find, and contain more varied remains, than those of bird-eating falcons such as peregrines or merlins. Kestrel pellets can be collected from nests or winter roosts. The latter are usually on buildings, straw-stacks or quarries, and are recognized by the white splash of droppings below the roost ledge. Kestrels' pellets measure about 25 × 15 mm (1 in × 0.6 in) and are distinctly tapered at one end. They can be stored for long periods if they are thoroughly dried (try a foil tray on a hot radiator — but beware of the smell) and protected from clothes moths (that will otherwise reduce your hard-won collection to a uniform dust!).*

*To examine pellets, pull them apart when dry, paying particular* attention to the small fragments of bones, teeth or bits of insect. Kestrels digest their prey much more thoroughly than do owls, so don't be surprised if some pellets contain just a few teeth. Bird remains are often ground to a fine powder with only the odd bone or feather barbule to show what they are. Mammals can be identified using reference guides (see Yalden [1977] in the Bibliography), while insects often leave distinctive legs or jaws. Earthworm remains are the yellow, S-shaped bristles or 'chaetae' that are often found if there is soil in the pellet, though you will need keen eyes or a magnifying glass to spot them.

The easiest way to quantify your results is to record the presence or absence of items in each pellet you sample. The results are then expressed as the percentage of pellets containing voles, shrews, birds, earthworms, etc. This does not show how many voles or shrews were eaten, but you may be able to detect changes in frequency between, for example, pellets collected in different months at the same winter roost.

Peregrines feed on birds, and their power and agility enables them to attack anything from a goldcrest to a greylag goose. The range of species known to have been taken is enormous — 132 in Britain and 210 in central Europe — but peregrines normally concentrate on birds between the size of starlings and domestic pigeons. Female peregrines probably take prey in the range 100 g-1 kg (0.2-2.2 lb), while their smaller mates work down the range at 20-200 g (0.7-7.1 oz). However, there is considerable overlap, and each sex can take prey well outside these limits.

Despite this variety, British peregrines are primarily pigeon-eaters. Domestic pigeons, or their wild ancestor the stock dove, are a major item on the menu at nearly all eyries, even those in remote uplands. Most of the kills are racing pigeons, which are released in millions every weekend during the racing season (April to September). Some fail to return home because they fly too slowly through a peregrine's territory, and pigeons account for 50-80 per cent of prey items at inland eyries in Wales, northern England and south Scotland. Pigeons are less frequent in areas away from flight-lines, where other prey become important. These include grouse in the eastern Highlands and seabirds at some coastal sites.

In all areas, summer prey of secondary importance include breeding waders (lapwing, golden plover, snipe and redshank) and passerines (especially starlings, blackbirds, song thrushes, skylarks and meadow pipits). Peregrines are no respecters of other raptors either, and occasional

*Male peregrine eating a pigeon.*

items include kestrels, merlins and short-eared owls. During winter, when the pigeon supply dries up, inland peregrines take more passerines such as redwings and fieldfares, while those on the coast take mainly feral pigeons and waders.

Many peregrines in the uplands rely on food that is just 'passing through' the area, rather than on those that live there permanently. This includes some waders and racing pigeons in summer, and migrant

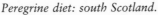
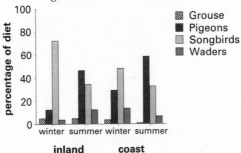

*Peregrine diet: south Scotland.*

*This graph summarizes data collected over several years by Richard Mearns in south Scotland. In this area, peregrines rely mainly on pigeons during the breeding season and on songbirds (especially redwings and fieldfares) in winter. Diet in coastal and inland areas is similar during the breeding season but peregrines wintering inland take mainly songbirds while those on the coast also take pigeons and waders. The diet thus reflects the relative abundance of the different prey groups.*

thrushes in winter. This might explain why density and breeding success is so high in these apparently impoverished areas, and how pesticides applied in low ground can find their way into distant peregrines.

**Merlins** also eat mainly birds, but they are at the smaller end of the market. A 'jack' (male) merlin would be unwise to tackle a large pigeon in full flight, even if he could catch up with it! Once again the range of species is enormous, but one or two items comprise the bulk of the diet. In one Northumberland study, breeding merlins took 50 species of bird, but meadow pipits accounted for over half the prey items found. Most prey weighed 10-40 g (0.4-1.6 oz), though there were a few eggar moths and some birds as large as fieldfares, plovers or feral pigeons. Nearly all were open-country species, and this was also true in Wales and Galloway, where meadow pipits, skylarks, starlings and wheatears made up 87 per cent and 72 per cent respectively of all bird items. In Galloway, merlins breeding in young conifer plantations seemed to shun woodland prey and flew out to moorland up to 4 km away to find food. This does not mean merlins are unable to adapt to different prey: city-dwelling merlins in the Canadian Prairies clobber the local sparrows, which make up three-quarters of the diet. Their rural neighbours, meanwhile, make do with native species such as horned larks or longspurs.

**Kestrels** take a much wider range of prey than the other falcons, though

'Perhaps Pigeons are too big' thought Jack

they are mainly hunters of small mammals. Hovering is ideally suited to catching small beasties running around in the grass, particularly short-tailed voles. Other mammals up to small-rat size are also taken, including shrews whose reputed foul taste makes no difference to kestrels with their poor sense of smell. Voles make up the bulk of the diet in grassy areas, but small birds may be important elsewhere, especially in summer when unwary fledglings are easy meat. Again, open country species such as meadow pipits and skylarks predominate.

In autumn and winter kestrels supplement voles and birds with smaller prey such as beetles and earthworms. These slower moving prey are especially favoured by young kestrels learning to hunt, and earthworms are easily spotted in pastures when they come to the surface in warm, wet conditions. But this by no means exhausts the list of recorded prey, which includes seasonal items such as lizards, as well as outright oddities such as crabs, fish and large black slugs!

The kestrel's wide distribution reflects its ability to take alternative prey when voles are scarce or absent. In Ireland, where there are no short-tailed voles, kestrels eat mainly woodmice and birds, while in cities and towns they take sparrows, starlings and young pigeons. Kestrels in southern

Europe take more lizards, birds and grasshoppers, and fewer mammals and beetles than their northern counterparts.

**Hobbies.** If kestrels are the generalists among falcons, then hobbies are the specialists, though even they take a variety of birds and insects. A study in southern England recorded hobbies eating about 20 bird species over 4 years, but over 50 species have been recorded elsewhere in Europe. The bulk of the food comes from birds caught in mid-air, especially hirudines (swifts, swallows and martins), sparrows, finches and tits. In England, hirudines were taken by hobbies feeding their young, and the parents may time breeding so that the nestling stage coincides with the fledging of swallows and swifts. Sparrows seem to be important prey near human settlements, and a long-term study in Berlin found they made up half the bird items taken.

Hobbies are also noted for taking large flying insects, especially dragonflies which they hawk over ponds and damp areas. But they also take beetles, chafers, moths and even small insects such as flies and ants. Although insects may be taken in April or May, hobbies only hunt for them if the temperature is above 13°C, presumably because few insects are on the wing below this temperature. Hobbies take mainly small birds early in the year and insects tend to be more important later in the season. In summer hobbies hunt well into the evening, even by moonlight, and their aerial agility is sometimes tested to the limit in catching bats.

*Hobbies frequently eat large dragonflies.*

Our four falcons thus reduce direct competition for food by specializing in different prey. There is still some overlap because all species take small birds such as meadow pipits or skylarks, and all are capable of taking advantage of an unusually abundant food source. For example, peregrines in the Canadian Arctic breed at high densities and rear large broods by exploiting lemmings during plague years.

Falcon Facts 3: **Main prey items**

This table is based on what is normally eaten during the breeding season in Britain. The star-rating (∗) shows the usual prey; 'o' = eaten occasionally, '–' = not eaten. The winter diet varies slightly from this, kestrels in particular taking more insects and earthworms than during the summer months.

| | Peregrine | Merlin | Kestrel | Hobby |
|---|---|---|---|---|
| **Mammals** | | | | |
| Rodents/shrews | o | o | ∗∗∗ | o |
| Bats | – | – | o | ∗∗ |
| **Birds** | | | | |
| Pigeon-sized | ∗∗∗ | – | o | – |
| Skylark-sized | ∗∗ | ∗∗∗ | ∗∗ | ∗∗∗ |
| **Lizards** | – | – | ∗ | o |
| **Insects** | | | | |
| Flying | – | ∗ | o | ∗∗∗ |
| Crawling | – | o | ∗ | ∗∗ |
| **Earthworms** | – | – | o | – |

# Standing out in the crowd

A number of biologists studying bird-eating falcons have noticed that they take unusual or bizarre items more frequently than would be expected by chance. In Holland and Germany, escaped budgerigars frequently turn up as hobby kills, and sparrows with albino flight feathers are taken more often than their distribution in the population predicts. Similar observations have been made for urban merlins in Canada, and for peregrines, which have been blamed for selectively killing rare breeding birds or unusual migrants that pass through their territories.

The budgerigars and sparrows may have attracted attention by their bright plumage, and other species may have odd flight patterns or behaviour. Perhaps falcons are demonstrating a natural curiosity shared with Victorian naturalists and some modern hunters who are inclined to shoot unusual animals just to see what they are!

# Bringing home the bacon: hunting

The hunting behaviour of falcons probably generates more interest and excitement than any other aspect of their biology. After all, hunting is what these birds are adapted for and why they have had such a long association with humans. This is particularly true of the peregrine, and the literature abounds with tales of its hunting prowess and speculation on how it kills its victims, at what speed and with what success. Despite this attention, we actually know more about the less glamorous hunting of kestrels, thanks to painstaking studies over the last decade or so. Merlins and hobbies are difficult to follow, and there are comparatively few studies of their hunting success.

The hunt has several stages: searching, attacking and 'disposing'. The disposing may be eating, taking it to the nest or storing it for later consumption. The two main ways of searching for food are either to fly

*Merlin splitting a flock.*

*Hobbies are agile enough to catch swallows and house martens.*

around and look for it or to sit and wait for it. The sit-and-wait approach is favoured by peregrines, especially those with high cliffs that give a good view. Perched peregrines can often be seen scanning the sky above, looking for passing victims that may be almost invisible to human eyes.

Searching by flying is more energetic, but can be more rewarding. This is true for kestrels, and for hobbies chasing insects. Peregrines, on the other hand, do less well by 'waiting on' in the air, perhaps because their prey can see them more easily and so have time to take evasive action. The mode of flying during hunts varies considerably: peregrines mainly soar, kestrels usually hover, merlins dash low over the ground, and hobbies fly back and forth over the same patch when taking insects.

The basic method of attack is to dive very fast and hit or grab the prey with the talons. The details vary, depending on the relative positions of predator and prey at the start of the attack. Perched merlins, for example, usually go for prey near the ground, so they approach with a low, powered flight that ends in a rapid glide and a sudden swoop. Hovering kestrels make a series of descents over a fixed spot, ending in a steep dive. If the vole is not caught immediately, the kestrel will spread its wings and flail its talons in the grass, trying to trap the frightened creature in those deadly claws. Strikes at insects on the ground are more leisurely, the kestrel landing next to the beetle or earthworm and picking it up directly with the beak.

Peregrine attacks are the most spectacular of all. When a likely victim is spotted, a perched falcon takes off and climbs rapidly into the wind to get above its quarry. This may involve riding the updraught of the cliff, soaring on a thermal or making a wide, circling climb by powered flight alone. Once above the fleeing bird, the peregrine folds its wings and dives, raking the victim with open claws and knocking it out of the sky. This

*Peregrine attacking a woodpigeon.*

often kills the victim outright, though it may be finished off with a bite when it hits the ground. Should it miss, the peregrine will bank steeply, using its momentum to gain height for another dive. The falcon may 'bind onto' smaller prey, killing it in mid-air with a bite on the neck.

This sequence by no means exhausts the peregrine's repertoire, and it may attack from directly behind or even below. Once the bird is hit, the peregrine may swoop down and catch it before it reaches the ground. Some hunts over the sea or lakes end with the victim being driven into the water before it is scooped up and killed by its tormentor. In another variation, called 'ringing-up', the peregrine drives its prey upwards by a spiralling flight, hoping to get it away from the safety of the ground before climbing above it and delivering the *coup de grâce*.

# Guess the speed of the peregrine

*This is a favourite game for falconers; competitors range from the 'think-of-a-number-and-double-it' brigade to the A-level physics buffs who cover the backs of envelopes with calculations and then double the number they first thought of! Maximum speed for level flight is consistently estimated around 100 kph (60 mph), but estimates for dives vary from less than 160 kph (100 mph) to over 430 kph (270 mph). The reason for the disparity is that conventional calculations rely on knowing the altitude of the bird at the top and bottom of the dive, the angle of descent and the time spent diving, none of which are easy to measure accurately.*

*Mathematical calculations based on the size of peregrines suggest a maximum terminal velocity of about 380 kph (240 mph), but is this ever reached? The most accurate estimates to date were made using a tracking radar, which recorded the height and distance moved during two dives made by a migrating peregrine in Sweden. The estimated speed was 90-140 kph (57-88 mph), quite a bit slower than many previous estimates, and about the same as dives measured elsewhere for hobbies. With such a small sample it is difficult to tell if these speeds are really representative of maximum possible values. Two suggestions for the relative slowness of dives are either because it improves accuracy when prey is struck, or that it reduces the enormous gravitational forces as the falcon pulls out of a dive and begins to climb.*

## The victim strikes back

Attacking falcons do not have it all their own way, and most birds and mammals have developed counter-measures to evade capture. A common trick is to 'freeze' as soon as the falcon is seen, and remain motionless until it passes by. A falcon's vision is probably not merely a magnified version of our own, but seems to be particularly sensitive to the movement of small objects. Birds or rodents on the ground can escape detection altogether by not moving, and I have watched kestrels perch above motionless sparrows for fifteen long minutes before they flew away, unaware of the meal they had just missed. This tactic is no use for flying birds, whose main hope is to outpace the falcon or reach the safe haven of a thick bush or hedge. Small birds will dive for cover if they are near the ground, while pigeons and other fast fliers will change up a gear and try and get away quickly. Even peregrines have difficulty in outpacing a pigeon in level flight.

The classic avoidance behaviour for flocking birds is to close up into a tight bunch in mid-air. This can produce spectacular displays of flock co-ordination, especially when peregrines or hobbies appear near starling roosts at dusk. Falcons are reluctant to dive into tight flocks, possibly because of the risk of injury, so they swoop near the edges and try to pick off stragglers.

## Hunting success

This is measured by following individual falcons for long periods and recording how often they make attacks and kills. This is not easy for bird-eating falcons that cover large areas, and the most reliable information comes from studies of kestrels. Success is often measured as the proportion of attacks that result in kills, but a more meaningful figure is the number of kills per unit time, or 'hunting yield'. The difficulty with this is deciding whether or not the bird is hunting; including times when it is not will make the bird seem less effective than it really is.

Not surprisingly, kestrels hunting insects have much higher success rates than those taking larger prey. They also catch voles more easily than birds, mainly because they are not specialist bird-feeders and many attacks fail. One exception is when kestrels are taking recently fledged birds that are unable to escape as easily as adults. Hovering is a better way of catching voles than perching, typical yields being 2-4 voles/hour compared with less than 1 vole/hour for active hunting from perches. Hunting success also varies with age, and juvenile kestrels in their first few weeks seem to make many unsuccessful strikes. It seems they must learn to

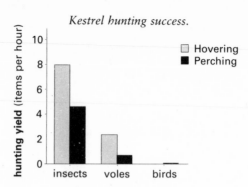

Kestrel hunting success.

*Kestrels hunt by hovering or from perches. Hovering is used mainly for voles and it is more effective than hunting from perches. Kestrels are poor bird-hunters; attacks are made from perches or from high soaring, and few are successful.*

distinguish prey that is likely to be caught from that which is likely to escape.

Success for bird-eating falcons also varies, but the issue is complicated because they sometimes chase prey with apparently little intention of killing it. Such 'half hearted' hunting is frequent in peregrines, and may explain why some observers have recorded less than one in ten successful attacks. At least half the attacks are likely to succeed where the falcon is really 'keen'. This may not be so for merlins, which seem to have consistently low success rates (5-15 per cent), and may kill only if they can surprise their prey. This does not prevent them bringing home enough food to rear their families, perhaps because they have such an energetic hunting behaviour that involves a high rate of attacks.

### Cacheing behaviour

Once food is caught, it is usually eaten immediately or carried to the nest in the claws. However, it may also be stored and eaten later. Cacheing has been recorded in many raptors and was once thought to be an unusual behaviour, worthy of a note in *British Birds* or the local ornithological report. However, we now know that it is a regular and important behaviour in falcons that allows them to feed independently of when they hunt.

Cache sites vary: kestrels usually store on the ground at a prominent landmark such as a tussock of grass, clod or stone. Only larger prey are cached, and they are normally laid in the open rather than being carefully

# A problem shared is a problem halved . . .

The low success rate of merlins is probably related to the difficulty of surprising small birds in open country where visibility is good. To overcome this problem, merlins sometimes hunt in pairs or use other raptors to flush prey. Pairs worked together on about 30 per cent of hunts during one study in Iceland, and they had more success than when hunting alone. Merlins have also been seen with sharp-shinned hawks in North America, and with hen harriers in this country, apparently taking small birds flushed by the larger raptor. It may be no coincidence that there are several reports of extra males seen bringing food to merlin nests during the breeding season, a phenomenon known in other birds of prey that have difficulty in catching food.

# Fast food

Researchers in Holland used the cacheing behaviour of kestrels to measure the birds' food intake. When they saw a kestrel cache a vole, they found it, weighed it and then returned it to its hiding place. They then followed the kestrel until it returned to eat the vole, and measured how long it took to eat the kill. Repeating this for different-sized voles showed that there was a predictable but non-linear relationship between the weight of prey and the time it took to eat it. Thus a 10 g vole might be disposed of in about 2 minutes, but a vole twice that size would take three times longer. Using this relationship they were able to calculate the weight of all items they saw kestrels eating. By following individually radio-tagged kestrels for long periods they built up a detailed picture of food intake throughout the year.

hidden. Storing may allow birds to make use of sudden flushes of prey, and I once watched a kestrel cache five young rats in less than an hour when she found them wandering about in a recently harvested field. However, kestrels often cache single items, normally in the morning for retrieval before dusk. It seems the behaviour is primarily to provide a short-term backup in case bad weather or bad luck reduces hunting success. Caches are usually retrieved within twenty-four hours and the birds use landmarks to help them find their stores. Females will often store food that the male brings them during incubation, and peregrine nesting ledges may accumulate several items at a time.

# Economy-seven kestrels: saving energy

The kestrel is the only British falcon that normally hovers, and this makes it instantly identifiable. To many people a kestrel is a brief image flashing by on a tedious motorway journey. Others will have found more time to watch one hovering and to admire the amazing co-ordination required to ride an updraught on a blustery day. The wings, body and tail may be in constant motion, but the head remains perfectly still, allowing the bird to scan the ground below for the slightest movement. The Jesuit poet Gerard Manley Hopkins was deeply moved by this sight, and one of his best poems is called 'The Windhover':

> I caught this morning's morning minion, king-
>> dom of daylight's dauphin, dapple-dawn-drawn Falcon, in his
>>> riding
>> Of the rolling level underneath him steady air, and striding
> High there, how he rung upon the rein of a wimpling wing
> In his ecstasy! then off, off forth on swing,
>> As a skate's heel sweeps smooth on a bow-bend: the hurl and
>>> gliding
>> Rebuffed the big wind. My heart in hiding
> Stirred for a bird, – the achieve of, the mastery of the thing!

But few people admiring a hovering kestrel realize that they are also watching an animal whose behaviour has been finely selected to minimize energy expenditure. Hovering is an energetic activity (try flapping *your* arms for ten minutes and see how quickly you tire!), so kestrels don't hover unless they have to. In winter, when they have only themselves to feed, they can survive on 2-3 voles a day and hunt mainly from perches.

*Kestrels often hung along motorway verges.*

This is a slower way to hunt than by hovering, but it uses about one fifth of the energy.

When kestrels have to hover, they can save energy by holding their wings motionless, rather than having to flap them continually. To achieve this they must get lift from the wind, so you normally see them hunting on the windward side of hills or on updraughts around buildings or motorway embankments. Hovering with still wings in this way is aerodynamically equivalent to gliding, so humans finally caught up with kestrels when they invented the hang-glider!

Unlike hang-gliders, kestrels can stay aloft on calm days by flapping their wings, but they normally do so only if they have to. In winter, they stay perched when the day is calm, and hunt on the wing only when there is sufficient wind to create updraughts. In strong winds it takes considerable effort to keep position and, like sensible hang-gliders, kestrels seek shelter until the wind drops. In summer, a male kestrel with a full brood may have to catch over twenty voles a day, which is possible only by hunting on the wing. Some breeding males have to flight-hunt for up to five hours a day, sometimes without much assistance from the wind. Hovering for that long drains the body reserves, and many males lose weight when feeding chicks.

Kestrels have one other energy-saving trick, which was noticed only recently. Dutch scientists filmed a hovering kestrel and minutely analysed its movements by combining slow-motion photography with sophisticated computer technology. The kestrel was hovering in a blustery wind, but its head moved less than 6 mm (0.24 in) in any direction during the whole

How not to do neck-stretching exercises

ten-minute sequence. It beat its wings only intermittently, holding them outstretched in a glide between bouts of flapping. What the scientists noticed was that during the glide the kestrel allowed its body to be blown backwards by the wind, but its head remained completely still. To do this, of course, it had to stretch its neck, and when this had extended about 4 mm (0.16 in) it could go no further, so the wings began to beat again and brought the body forward, ready for another glide. The whole sequence lasted less than a second, but was repeated over and over again, with unbelievable co-ordination and accuracy. By gliding in this way, even for such short periods, it was estimated that the kestrel reduced its energy costs by as much as 44 per cent.

# Nesting sites

Falcons do not build a nest out of twigs or sticks because, like owls, they lack the necessary instinctive behaviour. All they can manage is to scrape a saucer-shaped depression into which they lay their eggs. This helps to stop the eggs rolling away, and gives a degree of comfort and insulation to the incubating bird. The inability of falcons to build a nest sets them apart from many other raptors such as hawks, buzzards and eagles, which can create huge structures which are added to each year by successive pairs.

Finding the right place to scrape a depression can pose quite a problem for a falcon. Ideally, a nest should be somewhere that is dry, offers space for the chicks and gives protection from predators or the excesses of the British climate (mostly rain, but very occasionally hot sunshine). Although they are capable of breeding anywhere that meets these basic requirements, most pairs choose from a fairly restricted range of site-types. This may limit the species' breeding range or density in some areas, or force some pairs to use less than ideal sites.

**Kestrels** are the least fussy nesters, and have been recorded in an amazing variety of sites. The most frequent are rock ledges, tree holes and disused stick-nests built by species such as crows, rooks or magpies. However, they will readily take to nesting on buildings and can often be tempted into using nestboxes or baskets that resemble crow's nests. In Orkney, where there are no foxes or stoats, kestrels even nest on the ground among stands of rank heather. In general, the sites used in any given area depend on what is most available: rock ledges in uplands or coasts, stick nests in conifers in parts of Scotland and tree holes in lowland England. Kestrels prefer nests that are at least 3 metres (10 feet) up, and tree holes that are 30-60 cm (1-2 feet) across but not too deep. Such holes often appear where a main branch has broken off the trunk, especially in ash trees which are prone to rot.

The kestrel's versatility is displayed at its best in towns. Their German name *Turmfalke* means 'Tower Falcon', earned by their long history of nesting on church steeples or other tall buildings. The nest may be inside the tower if there is access or on an outside ledge where debris has accumulated, such as behind a statue or in a disused gutter. Kestrels have kept abreast of the times, and sometimes nest in window boxes on high-rise flats. In Israel this has become a common practice in several towns, and home owners have to compete with aggressive male kestrels for the right to use their balconies!

The other falcons seem to have more specialized nesting requirements, though they will occasionally adapt to odd sites. **Peregrines** in Britain are normally associated with the tall, rocky cliffs of uplands or coasts. Some ledges on these cliffs are used year after year; a few have been used for hundreds of years by successive generations of peregrines. Many cliffs have several possible ledges that a pair could use, and there may be an alternative cliff nearby. They prefer more inaccessible cliffs and ledges that are recessed to give protection from rain and snow.

In recent years, as the peregrine population has increased, some pairs have taken to nesting on smaller cliffs and 'walk in' sites, that can be easily

# Decorum with the decorators

*Kestrels nesting in towns have had to learn to rub shoulders with humans and adjust to their strange habits. One pair in Birmingham happily began nesting in their usual site — a hollow steel girder high up on the side of a factory. They thought it a bit strange when poles and planks appeared around the girder, and workmen started walking past the entrance to the hole. But the female shrugged off this attention and began to lay her eggs. A few days later a man appeared with a brush, removed the eggs, painted the inside of the girder and then carefully replaced them. The female kestrel, who seemed unusually tolerant, soon flew back to her newly decorated home and proceeded to rear her family as if nothing had happened!*

reached without climbing. Their vulnerability is evident from the frequency with which they are robbed by humans or predators. Elsewhere in Europe, peregrines nest in the old stick-nests of crows or ravens, and it seems odd that British birds don't avail themselves of such safer sites. In fact, tree nesting has been recorded recently, and may catch on in some areas. Perhaps the habit is one that has to be learned and passed on from generation to generation.

In other parts of their range, peregrines have taken a cue from kestrels and moved onto the man-made cliffs we call skyscrapers. One pair achieved instant fame by nesting on the office of a Baltimore newspaper and their somewhat erratic progress made the headlines for several months. Some captive-bred peregrines have been released into the wild from nestboxes on skyscrapers in an effort to encourage the habit. If peregrines could adapt to using different types of site they could expand their range into lowland England, and who knows where they might end up . . .?

**Merlins** have two main nesting options: upstairs or down. The upstairs sites are in old crow's nests, usually in conifers or pines because these are the most common trees in their upland breeding grounds. The downstairs

*Merlins often nest in dense heather.*

option is to nest among heather, usually on a steep bank. A few pairs get the best of both worlds by nesting in heather that grows on the top of huge boulders. Merlins often nest in the same locations each year, though the actual site may switch between stands of heather and nearby crow's nests. In some areas, ground-nesting merlins are likely to suffer predation, so crow's nests are preferred if they are available. This caused headaches for one team of researchers in Northumberland, who found their merlins had begun to nest in the dense conifer stands of Kielder Forest. Finding disused crow's nests in these plantations is no joke, and sometimes the only way is to watch the merlins go into the nest by sitting and waiting . . . and waiting . . . and waiting . . .

**Hobbies** seem to have the most particular nesting requirements because nearly all pairs breed in disused crow's nests. Particularly favoured are sites in small clumps of trees in parkland or on heaths, or those in scattered trees along hedgerows. Most records are from nests in Scot's pines, but this may reflect a bias to recording in southern England, and hobbies will also use nests in deciduous trees such as oak, elm or beech. A few pairs use stick nests built by magpies, rooks or sparrowhawks, but there are no records of any other type of site being used in this country. An enthusiast in Berlin has managed to get his population to use artificial baskets, presumably because these are even better than the real thing. Crow's nests tend to disintegrate after being home to crows *and* hobbies, so the latter often look for a nest that was built the previous year.

Falcon Facts 2: **Nesting sites**

This table is based on the type of site normally used in Britain. The star-rating (∗) shows the usual sites; 'o' = used occasionally, '–' = never used. With kestrels, the most frequent type of site varies from place to place, depending on what is available.

| | Peregrine | Merlin | Kestrel | Hobby |
|---|---|---|---|---|
| **Ledges** | | | | |
| On cliffs | ∗∗∗ | o | ∗∗ | – |
| On buildings | o | – | ∗ | – |
| **Stick nests** | | | | |
| On cliffs | ∗∗ | – | o | – |
| In trees | o | ∗∗ | ∗∗ | ∗∗∗ |
| **Tree holes** | – | – | ∗∗ | – |
| **On the ground** | o | ∗∗ | o | – |
| **Nestboxes** | – | – | ∗∗ | – |

# Getting it together or staying apart?

All four falcon species tend to nest in the same places year after year. This is not surprising where the site is a permanent cliff or a large tree-hole, but even birds using stick nests seem to choose the same localities each year. Where these localities only ever contain one pair at a time, they are called 'nesting territories', and are often spaced at roughly equal distances across the landscape. In south Scotland, for example, peregrine eyries are about 5 km (3 miles) apart, on average, provided there is no gap in suitable nesting cliffs. This regular spacing occurs in merlins and hobbies, as well as in many other raptors, and seems to arise because pairs defend the ground around their nest and prevent others settling in the gaps. The distance between nests varies, probably in relation to the food supply in the area. Hobbies in southern England are spaced at 4-5 km (2.5-3 miles), while in the East Midlands the gap is nearer 7 km (4.4 miles), presumably because there is less food around.

Kestrels show less tendency to regular spacing, and the gap between pairs can vary enormously. This is partly related to the greater variability in their food supply, so that a territory that supports one pair in a poor vole year may have two or three in a good one. In some cases many pairs breed together in what is virtually a colony. For unknown reasons this is more frequent on the Continent than in Britain. There are several reports of colonies on French and German cathedrals, and one colony on a motorway bridge near Jena has nearly twenty pairs in some years. The variety of spacing patterns in European kestrels is repeated among other falcons, and colonial nesting is the norm in species such as lesser kestrels or Eleonora's falcons.

# Moving home

*The marking techniques described earlier have allowed biologists to tell how often particular birds use the same nesting site from year to year. The extent to which there are changes of occupants at sites from one year to the next depends partly on how many breeding birds* survive the winter and partly on how likely they are to move between sites if they do survive. Peregrines are long-lived birds that tend to stay on the same territory. Richard Mearns trapped peregrines at nesting sites in south Scotland from 1977 to 1981. Where he was able to distinguish the occupants of a cliff in successive years, there was a one in five chance that at least one partner would be a new bird in the second year. This gave a measure of the combined effects of mortality and movement on changes of occupants at nest sites. When individual birds were caught in successive years, about one in ten had moved to another site, which gave a measure of the effect of movement alone. I did the same thing for kestrels in my two studies in Scotland and England. Changes at sites were more frequent than in peregrines, over half the sites changing one or both birds in successive years. With individuals, about one in four moved sites between years, though changes were more likely early in life. The higher turnover of kestrels is partly expected because they are shorter-lived birds, so fewer will survive from year to year. Most kestrels that do change site move less than 2 km (1.2 miles) to their new homes, though females are inclined to go a bit further than males. Peregrines are likely to have to travel further if they change sites, and moves of over 20 km (12 miles) were recorded by Richard Mearns.

# Breeding seasons and laying dates

The business of producing young falcons occupies about half the year, and involves a similar sequence of behaviour to that found in many other birds. This sequence, or 'breeding cycle', begins with pairs coming together at the nesting site and beginning courtship behaviour. Pairs will often remain together for several years, especially where they are able to stay together at their breeding grounds through the winter. If one or both partners leave the area in winter, there is less chance that they will re-mate with each other the following year. During courtship the male feeds his mate so that she is eventually able to lay eggs. Once the clutch is complete, the female incubates, and is fed by her mate until the chicks are old enough not to need brooding or guarding. She then helps her mate to feed the nestlings. When the young leave the nest they continue to be fed by their parents for some weeks until they can fend for themselves.

The duration of the cycle is fairly fixed within a species, especially the incubation and the nestling stages which depend on how long eggs or chicks take to develop. Large species usually take longer than small ones, so whereas peregrines require about 70 days from laying to fledging, merlins need only 60 days. The time spent in courtship or feeding fledged young is more variable between pairs, and is adjusted to suit circumstances. For example, kestrels that pair late in the season spend less time courting than those that meet earlier.

Throughout the breeding cycle, a major preoccupation of the pair is finding enough food to keep their breeding attempt going. Food is scarce in early spring, so the female may have difficulty in getting sufficient to lay eggs. Food is more plentiful in summer but demands are greater because the male must provide for himself, his mate and his young brood. Another critical time is when chicks become independent: young falcons may not survive their first few traumatic weeks unless food is plentiful and easy to catch.

**The timing of breeding.** Although food can be scarce in summer, pairs would have no chance at all of breeding successfully if they tried to rear chicks in winter or early spring when there is never enough to feed a brood. They must adjust breeding so that the young hatch at the right time of year, preferably as early as possible to give them a chance to learn to

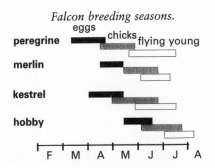

*Falcon breeding seasons.*

*The breeding cycle takes longer in large species than in small ones, so peregrines have to begin to breed early in the year to fledge young at the same time as merlins. Timing also depends on food: hobby prey is not abundant until late in the year, so they begin laying much later than the other similar-sized species.*

cope before winter arrives. The trick is to anticipate the time when food is abundant by beginning to breed well before this happens. In this way, chicks hatch as soon as the food supply will support them.

The timing of the laying season in our falcons thus depends how long they take to rear their young and when their main food first becomes abundant. Peregrines have a long breeding cycle so they must begin to breed early in the year in order to fledge young at the same time as the smaller falcons. Their laying period thus starts 4-6 weeks before that of merlins in the same region. But timing also depends on food. Rodents become abundant sooner in the summer than do small birds or insects, so the three small falcons all have different laying seasons despite their similar size. Kestrels are earliest, merlins next and hobbies, which rely on insects, are last.

How do birds anticipate the summer flush of food? They cannot use food alone as a cue to breeding, otherwise some pairs would begin in autumn, when food is plentiful but about to become scarce, rather than in spring, when food is scarce but about to increase. Birds overcome this problem by using daylength to control their hormonal systems, and thus achieve breeding condition at the right time of year. The lengthening daylight of early spring stimulates centres in the brain, causing them to release hormones that control the growth of the sex organs. Once the laying season is over, the long days of midsummer cause different changes that ensure birds are unable to breed again until the following spring, whatever the food supply in autumn.

**Control of laying date.** Daylength and hormones ensure that falcons breed in the right *season*, but they do not determine the exact day on

---

Falcon Facts 4: **Duration of the breeding cycle**

The duration of incubation is remarkably similar between the species, despite the range in size. The most striking difference is the longer time taken by peregrines to rear their young to independence, compared with the smaller falcons.

|  | Peregrine | Merlin | Kestrel | Hobby |
|---|---|---|---|---|
| **Laying season** | mid March-early May | May-early June | mid April-early June | June-mid July |
| **Incubation (days)** | 28-33 | 28-32 | 29-33 | 28-31 |
| **Nestling stage (days)** | 40-46 | 28-32 | 27-32 | 28-34 |
| **Dependent young (days)** | 35-42 | 14-30 | 15-30 | 14-21 |

*The female is inclined to over-eat*

which laying begins. This varies enormously, even between pairs breeding in the same area. In kestrels, for example, early pairs may start laying in mid April, but the last pairs not until the first week in June, a difference of over six weeks. What determines when a particular female will lay? Most of the evidence we have comes from kestrels and points to food supply as being the critical factor.

During courtship, females stuff themselves with food and put on weight. In kestrels this gain amounts to 30-80 g (1-2.8 oz), or 10-30 per cent of normal weight, in less than three weeks. Some of the extra weight is due to the developing eggs, but most of it is fat and protein. These reserves remain after the eggs are laid and are an important backup in case the male fails to bring food regularly during incubation. Females that can't accumulate reserves don't lay eggs, and the pair fails during courtship.

The time at which females begin to put on weight, and thus when they lay, depends largely on the behaviour of the male. Those that can find food easily feed their female early in the season, and these pairs are the first to lay. Other males are unable, or unwilling, to deliver much food until later in the season, and these pairs lay late. This probably explains why the average laying-date of kestrels is earlier when voles are plentiful because males are able to increase their feeding rates sooner in the season than when voles are scarce.

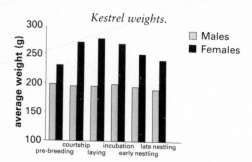

Kestrel weights.

*Female kestrels are larger than males so are heavier even in winter. However, during courtship the difference increases as females gain weight and remain heavy until the early nestling stage. Males stay the same until the nestling stage, when they lose weight because of the effort they put into feeding their brood.*

Food is likely to be the main factor affecting laying dates in the other falcon species, though there is much less evidence to prove it. Poor weather in spring is known to delay laying in peregrines, but this is probably an indirect effect of food supply. Wet weather makes prey species reluctant to come out of cover, as well as making it difficult for falcons to hunt. That climate is secondary to food supply is shown by the laying dates of kestrels in my two studies in Scotland and England: the Scottish birds were in good vole habitat and laid two weeks earlier, on average, than their English counterparts, despite the fact that they were further north and experienced colder, wetter springs.

# Fast breeders

*The effect of food on laying date has been demonstrated by experiments on kestrels in Holland and elsewhere. Researchers spent long hours during March and April visiting kestrel nestboxes to feed pairs with laboratory mice or day-old chicks. The dead food was left inside the boxes and the wild birds soon began eating it, thereby greatly increasing their daily rations.*

*Females that had extra food laid up to 2 weeks earlier than unfed birds in the same area, showing that shortage of food was delaying the breeding attempt under normal conditions. The difference between fed and unfed was much less during a good vole year, when some unfed pairs managed to find enough food to start early laying without the help of interfering scientists!*

# Breeding: the early stages

In order to breed a falcon must find a mate, somewhere to nest and sufficient food. Mates and nesting sites sometimes come in one package because single birds find a nesting territory and then look for a partner. We know little about how pairs get together because the first meeting is unlikely to be seen by any but the most ardent falcon-watchers. There is some evidence to suggest that it is often males who first acquire the nesting territory and then try to attract females to it. Males usually display to any females that wander into their territory, but females are more fussy. Adult female kestrels are more likely to mate with an adult than a first-year partner, suggesting they choose carefully rather than at random.

In sedentary populations, some pairs will have shared the same territory all winter, either because they paired the previous autumn or because they bred together the previous summer. In this case there is probably less overt displaying, and courtship behaviour will develop gradually as the breeding season approaches. Pairs that migrate separate in winter and are less likely to re-mate than are sedentary pairs. Whether or not a pair comes together again presumably depends on them both arriving at the territory at about the same time, before one of them finds another mate. Some migrant pairs manage to re-mate several years in succession, despite wintering separately hundreds or even thousands of miles away. Where most birds have to find new mates in spring, there is a great deal of display and fighting as birds jostle for precious nesting sites or mates.

Once the partnership is formed, courtship can begin. This is an important time for the pair, and several tasks must be successfully completed if eggs are to be laid. First, the pair must begin to work as a team, and establish the routines of behaviour that will make incubation go smoothly. Foremost is the feeding of the female by the male. This begins some weeks before laying, and gradually increases in frequency until the female stops hunting altogether and relies entirely on her mate. The food pass often takes place on or near the nest, usually at the same spot. The male signals his arrival by calling, and the female flies out to greet him, sometimes taking the prey in mid-air before he has a chance to land. Some males are reluctant to give up their hard-won food at first and might snatch back what they have just offered. However, most pairs have the exchange down to a fine art by incubation, and it runs like a well oiled machine.

*A mid-air food pass by hobbies.*

The second task is to defend the nesting territory, either from birds of the same species, or from potential predators. Although both birds will join attacks, the male does most of the aggressive displaying, and he is particularly vigilant against other males at this time. He has good reason to be: unattached males have been known to sneak in and try to mate with females who are left unguarded for too long!

A third job is to choose and prepare the nest. Most pairs have more than one place within their territory where they could lay eggs. For peregrines these may be different ledges on the same or a nearby cliff. Kestrels might have several empty crow's nests or tree holes to choose from, and merlins may have a ground site among heather and a crow's nest in a nearby tree. Preparation consists of scraping the material at the site into a smooth cup, a job probably done by both sexes. Pairs will often scrape several different sites, but the final choice seems to be left to the female, who sits in the scrape some days before she is ready to lay. If the nest gets wet, or she is constantly disturbed, she may change her mind at the last moment and go elsewhere.

The final tasks are to bring the female into breeding condition and fertilize the eggs. I have already mentioned the importance of courtship feeding in allowing females to gain weight and thus lay eggs. The rate at which males bring food increases steadily during courtship, and reaches a

Handy hints for nest-making N° 5 :
Bulldozing the nest-scrape

peak during laying. In kestrels this means males are bringing some 4-8 voles per day. The eggs are fertilized by copulations, but these start very early in courtship and are much more frequent than necessary for this function alone, so they probably also serve to strengthen the bond between the pair. The female solicits her mate by assuming a bowed posture and calling; he responds by flying to her and mounting from behind by fanning his wings rapidly. The whole process takes only a few seconds, and often follows a prey delivery.

The female becomes reluctant to fly as laying approaches and spends much of the day sitting on or near the nest. Such lethargy is common in many birds, and may help to protect the developing eggs from damage. In addition, females may gain weight faster if they avoid wasting energy in flying, though they are so heavy that flying may be difficult anyway.

### Calls and displays
Falcons have several ways of attracting or signalling to a mate, advertising territory-ownership or chasing away intruders. As with body-structure, the behaviour of falcons shows variations on a basic theme that has been modified and adapted by each species. The British falcons have similar displays and calls, though some species specialize in some types more than others. Aerial displays are related to flight-hunting skills, so they tend to

be most spectacular in peregrines and hobbies. Merlins have less spectacular displays, possibly because they hunt prey nearer the ground but also because they need to avoid drawing the attention of predators to the location of ground nests.

Flying displays between mates are highly varied, but there are three basic types:

**Flying together.** Pairs often soar together, sometimes to great height, and will swoop at one another in mock attack. Sometimes the lower bird will roll over on its back and briefly lock talons with its mate, mimicking aerial prey-transfers.

**Winnowing flight.** This is common near the nest when pairs are excited or threatened by intruders. The wing beats are shallow and rapid but flight is slow.

**Aerial displays.** These are performed high in the sky, visible for miles to other falcons but hard for bird-watchers to follow without getting a crick in the neck! They involve distinctive ways of flying that draw attention to the displaying bird, either to attract mates or to warn rivals. Chief among these are **rocking displays:** fast, horizontal flights in which the wings are flicked intermittently and the body rotates from side to side. Modified forms of this flight have been seen in peregrines, kestrels and hobbies, and may occur in merlins. Kestrels and hobbies make spectacular dives, or **V-flights** onto the nest, with the wings held upwards in a V-shape over the back.

Most of these displays are accompanied by calls which vary from species to species. All falcons call near the nest when breeding, but peregrines and kestrels seem to be noisier than merlins or hobbies. With merlins this may be related to the risk of predation at ground nests. Hobbies are noisy when they first arrive or when a nest of chicks is threatened, but are much quieter during laying and incubation.

**Alarm calls** are based on a single, repeated syllable which varies from 'kek-kek-kek' in peregrines through 'kee-kee-kee' in kestrels to 'kew-kew-kew' in hobbies. These calls are heard when humans or predators such as crows, magpies and raptors approach the nest.

**Trills** form a second set of calls, used mostly as signals between mates during displays and food passes. They are high-pitched, tremulous calls not unlike the begging calls of young chicks.

The **excitement call** is a single, short note often used by males as they approach the nest. It varies from a 'chup' in peregrines, to a 'tick' in merlins and a 'tisk' or 'kip' in kestrels and hobbies. There are several other calls which seem to be mixtures and variations of these basic types.

The pitch of notes varies with size, and may be lower in large females than in small males. Pitch also varies between species, and anyone who has heard all four falcons will recognize that they are using the same basic score: peregrines taking bass, kestrels tenor, hobbies alto and merlins the soprano line.

# Eggs and egg-collectors

The eggs are laid on alternate days, so a clutch of five takes nine days to complete. The female stays near the nest during this period, but she may not start incubating the eggs until at least three have been laid. The process of forming the eggs takes place in the oviduct over several days following the fertilization of the single egg-cell (ovum). This means that a female halfway through laying contains eggs at several stages of growth. The final stage is the production of the eggshell and its coloration by the brown pigments that give falcon eggs their distinctive appearance. Once the clutch is complete, any incompletely developed eggs are reabsorbed from the oviduct and the proteins used elsewhere in the body.

The number of eggs laid varies between species and between pairs of the same species. Large raptors tend to lay fewer eggs than small ones, though this rule can be overridden by the type of food eaten. Rodent-eating raptors usually have larger clutches than those that eat birds or insects, so kestrels normally lay 4-6 eggs, merlins 3-5 and hobbies only 2-3. Peregrines eat birds, but are larger than merlins, and normally lay 3-4 eggs. The variation between pairs of the same species is largely related to the time in the season when they lay: early pairs producing more eggs, on average, than late ones.

Falcon eggs are beautifully mottled with various hues of ruddy brown. The background colour ranges from almost pure white to a deep brown, and the degree of marking is also highly varied. The patterns overlap between species, so it takes an expert eye (and some luck) to identify the eggs of the smaller three species, which are similar in size. Peregrine eggs are instantly recognizable by their larger size, and were prized by collectors because of their varied colours and markings. Females seem to lay eggs of the same pattern from year to year, a fact suspected by egg-collectors and confirmed by scientists who were able to mark and identify wild birds. There is often variation in colour within a clutch because the

peregrine

hobby

kestrel

kestrel

merlin

merlin

5cm

2in

female's pigment supply gets depleted, making the last egg lighter than the rest.

Egg-collecting has passed its heyday, thanks to a more enlightened attitude among naturalists and some protective legislation. But it still goes on, and every year those who try to protect our falcons play a cat and mouse game with those who want to steal eggs. Egg-collecting began in Victorian times as part of the general craze for collecting and cataloguing specimens. It soon got out of hand: keen eggers were not content with one egg but wanted the whole clutch, and not one clutch but many. Some specialized entirely in peregrines, each year removing every egg from all the sites they knew. There is one famous photograph, taken in 1928, of two men standing proudly on a cliff-top in Dorset beside a pyramid of 64 peregrine eggs — their haul for that season alone!

The pastime became a mania to collect for its own sake and, although egg-collectors made many interesting notes, they must have severely depressed the output of young in some areas. This would have had less effect on long-lived species like peregrines than on merlins or hobbies, which must fledge more young to make up for the higher adult mortality. The collected eggs were carefully blown and stored in cabinets, row upon row, to be opened and ogled by their proud owners. And there the story would have ended, but for the unexpected intervention of pesticides in the 1950s. Suddenly, these collections became important sources of historical information which allowed scientists to show that the eggs of all falcons in Britain had undergone drastic shell-thinning after 1947, when DDT was first used. This does not justify the wholesale destruction of so many falcon nests, but at least the sacrifice had some beneficial side-effects in the end.

# Finding out eggs-actly what's going on

*Dutch researchers studying the process of egg formation in kestrels had to resort to cunning tactics to find out how long it took an egg to develop. They fed captive birds a special dye that was quickly deposited as a layer in the yolk of any eggs that were growing in the ovary. When the eggs were laid, the scientists hard-boiled them and carefully sectioned the yolk. By feeding the dye on different days, they could see which part of the yolk was laid down when, and therefore the rate at which the egg grew. The eggs developed from follicles in the ovary which were already 20 per cent of their final size some weeks before egg laying commenced. These follicles began to grow rapidly about nine days before laying, and were ovulated a week later. The last two days were spent in the oviduct having the albumen and shell membranes added.*

# Incubation

Because incubation begins about halfway through laying, usually with the third egg, the first two eggs do not begin to develop for several days and they hatch on the same day as the third. Eggs laid after incubation begins will be slightly behind the rest, so hatching in large broods is spread over several days (called 'asynchronous' hatching), though it is still shorter than the laying period.

In all four species incubation lasts around thirty days, less variable than you might expect from the wide range in female body size. During the month or so that the eggs take to develop, the female spends virtually the whole time on or near the nest. She does most of the incubation, and she alone develops a proper brood-patch along her belly and chest. This patch of bare skin is rich in blood vessels, and transfers her body heat to the eggs. The male will cover the eggs while his mate eats the prey he has delivered, but he is unable to warm the eggs effectively, and rarely sits for

*Female peregrine incubating.*

Incubation can be a boring time for females

more than a few minutes at a time. However, the schedule seems to vary between pairs, and in peregrines and merlins some males seem to spend up to a third of the day on the nest.

The pattern of food exchange also varies between pairs, some males landing on the nest edge with prey, others calling the female off the nest from nearby. The speed of the changeover seems to depend on the weather conditions. Scientists devised a cunning way of monitoring incubation behaviour by packing a dummy egg with electronic sensors that recorded the temperature of the nest. The egg was put in a peregrine nest in Scotland in early April, and it sent continuous radio signals that were picked up by receivers in a caravan about a mile away. The armchair ornithologists, sitting cosily by their monitors, could tell when a bird was off the nest by the sudden drop in egg temperature. On warm days the pair were fairly casual about leaving the eggs exposed, but during a sudden snowy spell they swopped over very quickly, the male shuffling up to the female and practically pushing her aside.

Life is monotonous during incubation, but females can relieve the boredom by pecking at material around the nest or by standing up and turning the eggs. They do this with the side of the beak, using a sweeping motion that rolls the eggs and moves them around the nest. This seems to be important for egg development, possibly because it prevents the shell membranes from fusing and distributes heat more evenly. Eggs occasionally roll out of the scrape if the female is suddenly disturbed and leaves the nest too quickly. In stick nests this usually means they fall and break, but on ledges females will sometimes retrieve eggs by hooking them carefully back with the underside of the beak.

Provided she is well fed by her mate, the female will maintain her high body weight during incubation. Although she is relatively inactive, the need for her to maintain body heat during incubation means she must still eat regularly. Females that don't get enough food gradually lose weight and are likely to desert their clutches. This often happens during prolonged bad weather if males are unable to hunt effectively. Fat females can withstand a temporary shut-down of service better than thin ones, who soon leave their eggs and hunt for themselves if their mates don't bring home the bacon.

*Female kestrels: body weight and clutch desertion.*

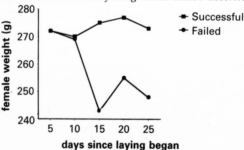

*By trapping female kestrels during incubation I was able to compare the weights of those that successfully hatched chicks with those that deserted their eggs. Both groups started at the same average weight, but the females destined to fail became progressively lighter as incubation wore on and eventually abandoned the nest.*

# Chicks in the nest

The young chicks can be heard calling from inside the eggs a day or so before they hatch. Soon after this, the eggs begin 'pipping' as the chicks bash a small hole using a special growth on the top of their beak, called the 'egg-tooth': a bad name because birds do not have teeth. Perhaps 'egg pick' would be better? It can take the chick another twenty-four hours to finally get out of the shell, and the whole process is as exhausting as labour in humans, except the newborn does all the work! The chicks are constantly brooded by their mother, drying their down into a white, fluffy coat.

Young falcons have partly closed eyes, but they are able to raise their heads and beg vociferously as soon as they sense they are being offered food. They wave their heads about, mouths gaping, tiny wings trembling and uttering a tremulous cheeping — behaviour which no self-respecting female falcon can resist. The male continues to deliver prey, which he passes to the female. She alone broods and feeds the young chicks, tearing the prey into tiny morsels, which she delicately offers in her bill. The chicks soon learn to take larger mouthfuls, but are usually over-ambitious in what they try to swallow. It is not unusual to see a chick with a bird's foot or mouse tail protruding from its beak, a tempting target for a sibling to try and steal.

Unlike some eagle chicks, falcon nestlings do not deliberately attack and kill one another under normal circumstances. They do compete vigorously for food, however, so the smallest chick is likely to get shoved aside if the going gets rough. This is where the asynchronous hatching helps. The last chicks to hatch are smaller than the rest and are the first to die if the brood is too large for the food supply. Not very helpful if you happen to be the youngest chick, but important for survival of the species! Chicks that die of starvation may be fed to their brothers and sisters or carried away from the nest by the parents.

The chicks grow very rapidly, doubling their birth weight in two days and reaching full size in 3-4 weeks. This rapid growth, among the fastest of any warm-blooded animal, is made possible by the high protein diet and because nearly all their food goes into growth, rather than maintaining body heat. Chicks are unable to control their own temperatures until about 10-14 days, and must be brooded by the female until then.

The different parts of the body grow at different rates, according to

*Peregrine chicks about three weeks old.*

what is needed at the time. Chicks are born with proportionately large heads and stomachs but tiny wings and feet. Their prime aim is to stuff food down themselves as quickly as possible, so the feeding apparatus is the most highly developed. A small chick is basically a down-covered intestine, highly efficient at converting dead meat into falcon meat! Later they must feed themselves, holding prey in their claws like an adult, so the feet and skeleton develop next. At the same time they must be able to control their body temperature when the female stops brooding, so they replace the original down with a coarser one, which is then shed as the proper body-feathers grow. The wings are not needed until the birds leave the nest, so the flight and tail feathers are among the last to develop.

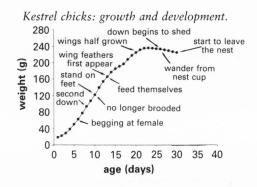

*Kestrel chicks: growth and development.*

*After a slow start, kestrel chicks grow rapidly from 5 to 20 days, when they reach adult size. Thereafter, growth concentrates in the developing flight feathers, and chicks actually lose weight before they leave the nest.*

The parents are kept busy delivering prey. At first the burden falls entirely on the male, and females only begin to hunt after they stop brooding, if then. By the time the female is hunting the young are able to feed themselves, so the male only has to sling the prey at them and leave quickly before he is mobbed by his hungry brood. The number of food deliveries depends partly on the size of the brood and the size of the prey. Peregrines deliver about 4-8 items a day, while kestrels may bring 10-20. While she is brooding, the female gives most of the food to the chicks, saving only the entrails and skin for herself. This causes her to lose weight during the early nestling stage, which may prepare her for hunting later on. She no longer needs fat reserves and carrying all that extra weight on hunting trips would be an unnecessary burden.

# Pushing kestrels to the limit!

*One question that has interested kestrel-watchers is whether or not the male can adjust the amount of food he brings to suit the needs of the brood. To examine this, Dutch researchers mounted a nestbox on the side of a caravan, which allowed them to watch the nest continuously from within. When the chicks hatched, they borrowed some extras from another brood and began rotating them in the nest, so the brood size remained constant but there were always hungry chicks in the nest. The male boosted his hunting effort, delivering up to 50 items on some days! However, he could not keep this up indefinitely because he was having to hunt for up to 8 hours a day, which used up more energy than he could replace from his food. To even things out, the researchers also tried the opposite experiment of providing extra food to the original brood, and the male was able to loaf about all day and only 'top-up' if necessary. Males were more likely to respond to the needs of their brood after the chicks were 10 days old, possibly because this is the time when they deliver food directly, rather than giving to the female, so they could tell more easily if the chicks were hungry.*

Small birds generally develop faster than big ones. Young peregrines are ready to leave the nest after 5-6 weeks and the smaller falcons after about 4 weeks. In peregrines and merlins, where there is a large difference in size between the sexes, males usually develop slightly faster than females and may leave the nest a few days sooner than their larger sisters. In kestrels and hobbies it is much more difficult to tell the sexes apart by size or plumage. By this time the juvenile body feathers are almost fully grown, and only a few wisps of down remain. The wing and tail feathers are not completely grown when the birds first fly, giving fledgling wings a more rounded appearance than those of adults.

Young birds can fly by instinct, but they have to wait until their muscles and feathers are sufficiently developed before they are ready to launch out. The first flights are usually short and downwards, and the landings decidedly dodgy. However, chicks that get stuck can call for their parents, who will deliver prey to them until they are able to haul themselves into a good spot for another takeoff. Falcon nestlings are particularly prone to leap from the nest prematurely if disturbed late in the nestling stage, and ringers have to take great care when visiting nests at this time.

Feeding rate experiment

later....

# Breeding ability

Measuring the breeding performance of raptors took on an added importance when it was realized that pesticides could lower their breeding success. This happens at levels much lower than those needed to kill birds, so such 'sub-lethal' effects of pesticides on breeding are an important clue to the health of the population. All raptor populations suffer some breeding failures; the questions of interest for biologists are whether these failures are unnaturally high and, if so, whether the species can compensate for the losses and still maintain its population levels. Even in healthy populations, only a few of the eggs laid result in birds that breed in the next generation, so increased losses before chicks leave the nest might be balanced by an increase in survival later in life.

The productivity of pairs is usually measured in terms of the number of young that leave the nest in a given year. This will depend on how many eggs are laid, how many of these hatch and how many of the chicks survive to fledging. The date on which the young fledge (which depends largely on the laying date) is also an important aspect because early fledged young are more likely to survive their first winter than those that leave the nest later in the season. So the most successful pairs are those that produce large broods early in the season.

## Causes of failure

Breeding is a long and complex process in falcons, and there is plenty of scope for getting it wrong. Well over half the pairs may fail to fledge chicks, and many of those that do succeed will lose some eggs or chicks along the way. Some pairs abandon breeding even before the eggs are laid. These are often referred to as 'non-breeding' pairs, though they may have scraped a nest and indulged in normal courtship behaviour. Others will manage to lay eggs but for various reasons will not hatch any chicks. Once they have chicks, the chances of raising young are better, probably because only the more competent pairs are left in the race by then; those that get that far usually have the ability to feed chicks to independence. Thus in kestrels, some 25 per cent of breeding failures occur before any eggs are laid, 62 per cent occur during incubation and only 13 per cent when there are young in the nest.

The actual causes of failure are many and varied, but they can usually be traced to a shortage of food, a poor nest site or human-induced failures

Falcon Facts 5: **Breeding performance**

Breeding varies from place to place and year to year. This table is based mainly on studies in Scotland and England, and gives average results for several years. Our knowledge of hobbies is very poor, and the figures are mainly from a study in Berlin. In most cases, only about half the pairs that start breeding are actually successful in fledging any young, and most failures occur before the chicks hatch.

| | Peregrine | Merlin | | Kestrel | Hobby |
|---|---|---|---|---|---|
| | South Scotland | North-umberland | Orkney | Scotland and England | England and Berlin |
| **Clutch size** | | | | | |
| Average | 3.5 | 3.3 | 3.9 | 4.6 | 2.9 |
| Min.-Max. | 3-5 | 3-6 | ? | 3-7 | 2-4 |
| **Brood size** | | | | | |
| Average | 2.3 | 3.3 | 2.5 | 3.6 | 2.3 |
| Min.-Max. | 1-4 | 1-5 | ? | 1-6 | 1-4 |
| **Young fledged/ pair** | 1.1 | 1.9 | 2.2 | 1.9 | 1.8 |
| **Percentage of pairs:** | | | | | |
| Not laying | 17 | 4 | 18 | 11 | 15 |
| Failing with eggs | 17 | 27 | 48 | 27 | 6 |
| Failing with chicks | 19 | 9 | 5 | 6 | 2 |
| Fledging chicks | 48 | 60 | 29 | 56 | 77 |

due to pesticides or the robbing of nests.

**Lack of food.** This is probably the most important cause of failure, and can arise for several reasons. The male may be a poor hunter, or have a territory with little food, so he does not deliver sufficient prey to his mate. She may fail to gain enough weight to start laying or, if she does, may desert her eggs because she can no longer wait for her mate to feed her. Starvation of chicks is another symptom of food shortage, though this rarely becomes so severe that all the chicks die. However, losses of some chicks from broods is not uncommon, usually because the smallest chick is underfed.

**Problems with nesting sites.** Some pairs nest in places that are less than ideal and suffer the consequences. Kestrels may lay eggs in stick nests that subsequently collapse, or in tree holes that flood after heavy rain. I once visited a brood of kestrels in an old crow's nest that had been used for several years and found all the chicks dead at the bottom of the tree. A

Some nest sites are safer than others ...

hole had developed in the middle of the nest which was just big enough for the half-grown chicks to fall through, one by one, as they moved around the nest. In south Scotland, peregrines nesting in sheltered ledges are more likely to fledge chicks than those at more exposed sites, implying that wet weather may directly kill older, unbrooded chicks. Pairs that use an unsuitable site probably have no alternative, though some may make a poor choice and others simply suffer bad luck as an otherwise good site is destroyed by chance.

**Nest robbing.** Predators account for a small number of failures in most populations, usually foxes or stoats attacking ground-nesting peregrines or merlins. Normally it is the nest contents that are destroyed, but a few failures result from the adults being killed. Peregrines have been known to cause failures at kestrel and merlin nests by killing and eating the adults. Crows may sometimes steal the unguarded eggs of smaller falcons, but usually only after the female has already deserted the clutch.

Human thieves can be a much more serious problem than natural predators in some areas, particularly for the rarer falcons. As with predators, pairs with the most accessible nesting sites are most at risk, but even a dangerous cliff may not stop a determined egg-collector or chick thief. In south Scotland, at least 17 per cent of failures among peregrines were due to robbery of eggs or chicks, and this amounted to almost one in ten of all breeding attempts.

Gamekeepers sometimes cause failures by destroying nests or killing the parents. This was probably a more widespread problem at the turn of the century, when gamekeeping was at its height. Nowadays it tends to be a localized problem and keepers are more likely to help falcons by deterring visitors, controlling predators and, for merlins, by improving the quality of heather moors.

**Pesticide-related failures.** The main problems are the thinning of eggshells and embryo deaths caused by DDT and other organochlorines. There is little detailed information as to how much failure this caused in falcons at the height of the pesticide era in the 1950s and 1960s. The best data come from records of peregrines. In south Scotland, almost 50 per cent of the pairs that laid in the early 1960s failed to hatch their eggs, but this had fallen to around 20 per cent by the late 1970s. A detailed survey from 1974-82 showed that about half these failures were because eggs broke or were addled, so pesticides by then were responsible for only about 14 per cent of all nesting failures.

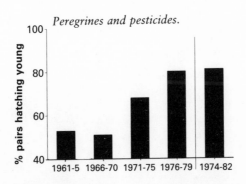

*Peregrines and pesticides.*

*Peregrines in south Scotland were severely affected by pesticides during the 1960s, with less than half the pairs hatching their eggs, often because they failed to lay or broke their eggs. Success has greatly improved with the withdrawal of DDT, and a detailed study in the area from 1974 to 1982 by Richard Mearns and Ian Newton confirmed the high hatching success indicated by the national survey.*

The different species of falcon seem to be vulnerable to different types of nesting failure. Non-laying, pesticides and robbery are important for peregrines in south Scotland, where there is little evidence that pairs with eggs suffer food shortage unless the weather is very wet. Kestrels, by contrast, are relatively unaffected by pesticides or robbery, but do suffer food shortage in incubation, causing females to desert their eggs. The extent and causes of failures in merlins varies from place to place, but they seem to be most at risk from pesticides, predation or robbery by humans. Poor food supply may also be an important factor, though it may act at an early stage in the breeding cycle, causing pairs to fail even before they lay eggs. There are few details for hobbies from this country, but in one German study the main causes were failure to lay eggs, pesticides and predation.

---

Falcon Facts 6: **Causes of breeding failure**

The different species are vulnerable to different problems during breeding. Peregrines show few symptoms of food shortage such as clutch desertion, but are prone to problems with pesticides such as egg breakage or addling and to human robberies. The opposite is true for kestrels. Merlins seem to be vulnerable to predators in Northumberland but to egg breakage in Orkney. Orkney eggs have rather low pesticide levels but high levels of mercury, which might be causing the problems. Once again there has been little systematic study of the causes of failure among hobbies. Some of the differences are due to the way the results were interpreted by the scientists: — predation is particularly difficult to identify, so some failures blamed on predators may have been due to humans or other causes.

| | *Peregrine* | *Merlin* | | *Kestrel* | *Hobby* |
|---|---|---|---|---|---|
| | South Scotland | North- umberland | Orkney | Scotland and England | England and Berlin |
| **Percentage of failures due to:** | | | | | |
| Non-laying | 33 | 11 | 9 | 25 | ? |
| Deserting clutches | 1 | 11 | 12 | 48 | ? |
| Egg breakage | 14 | 17 | 44 | 4 | ? |
| Human robbery | 17 | 11 | 3 | 1 | ? |
| Predators? | 5? | 48 | 24 | 8 | ? |
| Other causes | 30 | 2 | 8 | 14 | ? |

# Good times and bad times: variations in performance

The average breeding performance of pairs in an area can vary enormously from year to year, depending on fluctuations in the food supply and weather. The effect of changing food supply on breeding is most obvious in kestrels which lay larger, earlier clutches and suffer fewer failures in good vole years than in poor ones. In Finland, where vole numbers show marked changes from year to year, kestrels in one area fledged an average of 3.6 young per pair during a vole plague but none when vole numbers crashed.

Bird-eating falcons such as peregrines usually have a more stable food supply, so year-to-year variations usually depend on the weather, especially in the upland areas of Britain which tend to get more than their fair share of rain! Rainfall in May is crucial to the success of peregrines in south Scotland, and fewer than half the pairs will produce young in a wet year compared with over 70 per cent in a dry one.

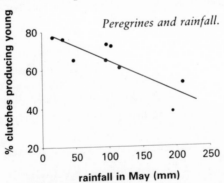

Peregrines and rainfall.

*These results are based on a nine-year study in south Scotland by Richard Mearns and Ian Newton. The wetter the May, the more likely peregrines were to desert their clutches or lose all their chicks.*

# Rain stops lay

The effects of changing food supply can be compounded by the weather, as I discovered to my cost in Scotland during 1976. Unlike England, which was gripped by drought, the May of that year was one of the wettest on record in my study area. In addition, vole numbers, which had been high over winter, crashed suddenly in spring. It was my first year studying kestrels, and throughout the month my mood matched the foul weather as nest after nest failed because the females deserted their eggs. By the end of the season, well over half the pairs had failed, and I was left with only 21 chicks to ring. Despite the poor start, I continued with the study. Two years later, when the voles were increasing again and the May rainfall was a tenth of that in 1976, I ended up ringing over 150 chicks!

## Super-pairs

Besides variations in *average* performance between years or areas, there is always a considerable difference between the productivity of pairs nesting in the same season. Some of this may be due to one pair having a better territory or nest site than another, but much also depends on the abilities of the pair themselves. Age has something to do with this, because pairings between birds in their first year are generally less successful than those where one or both partners is an adult. Presumably this is because first-year birds are not as experienced hunters as adults, though it may also be because they tend to end up with the poorest territories. Even among adults, however, some pairs fail while nearby pairs fledge large broods. They must share similar hunting areas, so their better performance must be due to their better abilities.

# Laying date and clutch size in kestrels – an interesting problem

The most productive pairs are those that lay early in the season. They tend to have larger clutches and are less likely to fail than late-laying pairs. This trend is seen in many bird species, and has puzzled ornithologists for years. After all, if food supply is gradually improving during the season, late laying pairs should have more food available when they lay, and ought to be able to produce more eggs. But the reverse is true — while early pairs are coping with the demands of a newly hatched brood, late pairs are struggling to lay any eggs at all.

There have been two main explanations for these observations, and kestrels have featured prominently in testing these theories. One idea says that late-laying pairs are such poor hunters that even the improving food supply is insufficient compensation. So they struggle to lay at all, can produce only a few eggs and are unlikely to make it through the breeding cycle.

This suggests that giving food to late laying pairs ought to boost their clutch size. However, work by Dutch scientists on kestrels suggests this may not be so. They prevented captive pairs from laying until late in the season, and then gave them as much food as they wanted. Even with the extra food, the late pairs still produced smaller clutches than the early pairs. The Dutch scientists suggested that evolution has linked clutch size to laying date because rearing large broods late in the season is inefficient: most of them will die anyway and a large brood puts an extra strain on the parents. They argue that the increasing daylength in late May and early June triggers hormones that prevent large clutches being laid. This mechanism cannot be broken by providing extra food, so clutch size depends mainly on when the female starts to lay, not on the food supply.

Neither theory fully explains all

*Kestrel breeding performance: effect of laying date.*

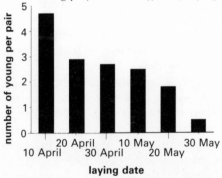

As in many birds, kestrels that lay early in the season are more productive than those laying later. This is partly because they lay more eggs, and partly because they are less likely to fail in their breeding attempt. Together these effects mean the first pairs to lay are ten times more productive than the last.

*the evidence available, so the jury is
still out on this question. However,
the kestrel's ability to breed easily
in captivity makes it an ideal*

*subject for this kind of study, and it
is likely to aid the final solution of
the problem.*

# Leaving home

If parents manage to rear chicks to fledging they then have to care for
them until they are ready to launch out on their own. This stage of the
breeding cycle is less well studied than the nest-stages, partly because it is
harder to record what is happening and partly, I suspect, because most
field-workers are worn out by this stage of the season! Nonetheless, the
first few weeks out of the nest are crucial for the young, who must quickly
learn to fend for themselves or face certain death as winter approaches.

### Post-fledging dependence
For a few weeks the parents continue to bring food to the chicks. At first
they carry it to the nest, so the young stay close by to ensure they get fed.
Feeding is on a first-come first-served basis, so there is a strong incentive
to grab food from parents as soon as they hove into sight. The young rush
out to meet the incoming meal as they become more competent at flying,
grabbing it in mid-air from their parent's talons. This can involve rolling
over onto their backs in a similar fashion to some of the aerial breeding
displays they may use later in life.

The chicks loaf about when they are not feeding, preening any
remaining down from their feathers and practising mock attacks.
Peregrines will chase their siblings or soar up and stoop at passing birds or
predators such as crows or buzzards. These attacks are more playful than
serious, but they have an important function. Predators such as falcons
must learn how to co-ordinate their hunting and accurately judge
distances if they are going to kill effectively.

Attacks gradually become more serious and are directed at easily caught
prey such as large insects. Anything moving on the ground is likely to
attract the attention of a young kestrel, and one was seen to dive at the
twitching ears of a full-grown hare that stood out from the cut stalks of a

Misdirected attacks Nº 3 : A Merlin would
be ill advised to tackle a Mute Swan

stubble field! Young peregrines dive at tussocks of grass and even clumps of seaweed floating in the water.

The transition to full independence is gradual and may take up to 6 weeks in peregrines or 3-4 weeks in the other species. Exactly when the young leave probably depends on when the parents stop feeding them. Kestrels that fledge early broods feed them for up to 2 weeks longer than do the parents of late broods, and this may enhance the survival of early young. With the sparrowhawk, a similar bird of prey, juveniles will stay near the nest for weeks beyond the normal date if they are artificially fed, so dispersal is probably triggered by the need to hunt rather than the young being driven away by their parents.

# Trained killers

Peregrine-watchers have long claimed that some parents teach their fledglings to hunt, either by deliberately dropping prey for the young to catch in mid-air, or by bringing back live prey and releasing it just as the young are about to grab it. Falcons normally kill their prey before they carry it, so bringing live prey implies a deliberate action, rather than an accident. Parents may also help their young by flushing prey or chasing it to exhaustion so that the young can easily catch it.

Hand-reared falcons can be released into the wild by providing food at feeding stations and gradually letting them learn to hunt for themselves. This shows that young birds do not have to be taught to hunt, but lessons from parents may give a vital edge to wild birds who do not have the luxury of time to learn.

## Dispersal from the nest

When the moment comes to leave, the young falcons seem to move off in a more or less random direction. This is true even for those that later migrate, and systematic movements in a particular direction are not usual until September or October. Most young do not go far at first, and kestrels ringed as nestlings are usually recovered within 75 km (47 miles) of the nest during July and August. A few intrepid individuals will move away rapidly, however, and one ringed kestrel turned up 300 km (186 miles) from its nest less than a month after fledging. Most birds probably travel alone, though some ring recoveries suggest that nest mates might sometimes stay together. I found two sibling kestrels on adjacent winter territories some 20 km (12 miles) from their birthplace, an event that was unlikely if they travelled independently.

The priority for dispersing birds is to find a territory where they can live during winter. Early fledged birds probably find plenty of space when they disperse, and can settle near to home. Late leavers will find it increasingly tough to find a home, and there is much territorial fighting by both sexes in early autumn. This might explain why early fledged birds settle nearer to their birthplace while late-comers are driven on to more distant wintering grounds. This effect continues after the first winter, and early fledged birds are also more likely to breed near to where they were born than are late ones. Late fledged young are often unable to overcome the

*Young chasing adult peregrine.*

disadvantages of their poor start in life, and are more likely to die in their first winter than are young from early broods.

Young peregrines are inclined to wander widely in search of a new home, and sometimes turn up well out to sea. One landed on a ship 1,300 km (800 miles) off the West African coast, still only halfway to South America. It is perhaps this wide dispersal of juveniles, rather than their migratory habits, that have given the species its Latin name *peregrinus* or 'wanderer'.

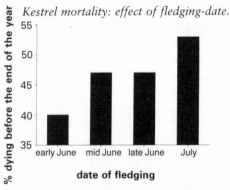

*Kestrel mortality: effect of fledging-date.*

*Examination of the BTO ringing data shows that kestrels fledged early in the season are more likely to survive to the end of their first calendar year than the young of broods that do not leave the nest until July.*

# Peregrinations: migrations

Migrations are distinguished from the 'random' dispersal of juveniles by being more systematic movements between breeding and wintering areas. The four species of British falcons are totally migratory in those parts of their range where there is permanent winter snow cover but are mostly sedentary in milder areas where the winter food supply is more predictable. Britain falls between these extremes, and our falcons display a range of migratory behaviour that reflects their differing abilities to cope with winter weather.

British peregrines and merlins show only weak migratory behaviour, and most birds probably winter within 75 km (47 miles) of their nesting areas. Those breeding in the uplands face a shortage of food in winter as most small birds move to low ground and, for peregrines, the pigeon racing season comes to an end. Both peregrines and merlins are found mainly on low ground in winter, particularly along coasts and marshes where waders and flocks of finches are abundant. Some peregrines may even move into cities to feed on pigeons, and single birds have roosted on St Paul's Cathedral. First-winter birds are more likely to migrate some distance, especially merlins, and there are a few long-distance recoveries of British-bred merlins from south-west France and Spain.

Kestrels are more vulnerable to cold weather than are bird-eating falcons because their ground-dwelling prey becomes unavailable if covered by thick snow. In northern England and Scotland kestrels are partial migrants, some of the breeding population moving south-east in winter and others staying behind. Not all birds go far, and many winter in the farmlands of central and eastern England. However, both adults and juveniles occasionally cross the Channel and join the generally south-westerly movement of kestrels from north-east Europe and Scandinavia. Some British kestrels probably go as far as West Africa, though the farthest recoveries to date are from Morocco.

Kestrels are mainly sedentary in southern and central England, and breeding pairs show little consistent migration. This means that northern birds move further than southern ones, though most still spend the winter north of a line between Anglesey and the Wash. In parts of Scandinavia there is a true 'leap-frog' migration, with birds from the far north wintering further south than those from southern Sweden and Denmark, which mostly stay put.

Hobbies feed on prey that is unavailable in Britain during the winter. Swallows and swifts migrate to Africa, adult dragonflies die and bats hibernate. So hobbies are true migrants, leaving our shores in autumn and travelling all the way to Africa. As far as we know, they spend the winter south of the equator in countries such as Angola, Namibia and Zambia. However, so few hobbies have been ringed, and recoveries of any birds from Africa are so unusual, that the most southerly British recovery to date is from Portugal.

### Britain: land of winter sunshine?

Although our winter climate may seem to have little to commend it, it is a considerable improvement on places such as Iceland and Scandinavia. So Britain regularly plays host to migrant falcons from elsewhere. Peregrines will come from Scandinavia, whereas visiting merlins come mainly from Iceland. Ringed kestrels have been found to originate in a variety of countries from Finland to France. Most recoveries are Dutch birds, but this may reflect the large number of kestrels ringed there, compared with surrounding countries.

### When they go

The only detailed information on the timing of migration in British falcons comes from kestrels. The other three species have fewer ring recoveries

Falcon Facts 7: **Movement of ringed birds**

This table is based on an analysis of the BTO ringing data up to and including 1990.

|  | Peregrine | Merlin | Kestrel | Hobby |
|---|---|---|---|---|
| Number ringed | 4,544 | 7,728 | 36,658 | 716 |
| Number recovered | 383 | 544 | 3,342 | 26 |
| % Recovered outside Britain | 1% | 5% | 6% | 15% |
| Longest distance (km) | 1,712 | 2,024 | 2,591 | 1,283 |
| From: | Co. Antrim | Grampian | Northumbria | Wiltshire |
| To: | Portugal | Spain | Morocco | Portugal |
| Number of foreign-ringed birds recovered in GB | 12 | 25 | 82 | 2 |

and, in the case of peregrines and merlins, do not show such marked migrations. Kestrel migration gets under way in early September and finishes in late October. Juveniles seem to start moving before adults, and generally migrate longer distances. In spring the reverse is true, and adults arrive first on the breeding grounds. This may be because they are keener to find a breeding territory, have less far to go, or possibly because their better hunting abilities enable them to survive on the breeding areas early in spring when the weather is still unpredictable. Migrating birds may also use different routes according to their age. In America, first-winter peregrines migrate down the Atlantic seaboard while adults prefer the inland route along the Appalachian Mountains.

The behaviour of falcons during migration is hard to study, but our knowledge has been greatly increased by radio-tracking. One enthusiast in America tagged a young male peregrine in Wisconsin and followed it as it made its way to Mexico. The bird would hunt in the morning for about three hours and then migrate during the middle of the day. It usually stopped to make a second kill about two hours before sundown. Progress depended on the weather, the bird covering over 320 km (200 miles) on fine days with a following wind, but hardly moving at all when it was heavily overcast and raining. In 15 days the young peregrine covered 2,634 km (1,637 miles), at an average speed of 35 kph (21 mph) or 188 km (111 miles) a day. His dedicated followers finally gave up at the Mexican border when their money ran out and they had difficulty explaining to border guards what they were doing!

# Winter thermals

*Many raptors use hot-air thermals during migration to avoid the need for energy-sapping flapping flight. Broad-winged hawks, such as buzzards, eagles and sparrowhawks soar to the top of one thermal and then glide to the bottom of the next. This sort of*

*Black storks and hobby over Bosphorus.*

flight is difficult over water because there are few thermals, so these species converge in great numbers at short sea crossings such as the Straits of Gibraltar or the Bosphorus. Falcons do soar on migration but they are not totally dependent on thermals and they are able to make long sea crossings. This means they can migrate on a 'broad front', rather than along narrow routes, so fewer falcons are seen at the concentration points on migration routes.

Kestrels regularly cross the North Sea, a distance of over 400 km (250 miles), and are seen on oil rigs in spring and autumn. The crossing must require many hours of continuous flight, but pales to insignificance compared with some other falcons. The record for regular over-sea migrations must go to the eastern red-footed falcon, a hobby-like species that breeds in Siberia but winters in South Africa. Each year it crosses the Indian Ocean without stopping, a distance of some 3,000 km (1,800 miles)!

# Life in winter

Survival is the name of the game in winter, and the migrations of falcons to wintering grounds have evolved because they increase the likelihood of individuals staying alive until spring. But reaching another spring is no use, in evolutionary terms, if an individual doesn't breed again, so falcons face an additional pressure of ensuring they get a nesting site when winter ends. This probably explains why some birds try and brave the weather by staying on their breeding territories all winter.

Pairs remain together on their territories in mild areas, but may separate where winters are more severe. In the uplands, kestrel pairs separate in winter, and it is often the female that moves away and the male who stays. This has been observed in Canadian merlins, and may be because it is the male who has to establish the breeding territory next spring and who has more to lose by giving it up in winter. British peregrines seem to stay together at the nesting cliffs for much of the time, moving to nearby low ground only if the weather deteriorates. A survey of peregrine nesting sites during one winter in south Scotland found that over 80 per cent were occupied by at least one bird.

## Winter habitats

Juveniles are unlikely to breed the following spring but they are likely to starve in winter, so they have more incentive than adults to spend the winter where food is plentiful, even if there are no breeding sites. In the Scottish peregrine study just mentioned, 80 per cent of the peregrines seen on low ground in winter were juveniles, whereas all the birds at upland breeding sites were adults. In my upland study area in Scotland, first-year kestrels were present in winter when voles were abundant, but moved away in a poor vole year, when only adult males remained.

A study of merlins in Galloway suggested that birds of all ages wintered mainly in lowland farming areas, rather than along coasts, as is often supposed. Males did not seem to select different habitats to females, nor juveniles to adults, though adult females are hard to distinguish from juveniles, so some segregation may have gone unnoticed. In American kestrels, the sexes can be easily distinguished in juveniles making study of habitat selection easier than in merlins. Studies in various parts of the species' winter range have shown that females of all ages seem to prefer open habitats, while males are usually found in more wooded areas. Females tend to arrive on the wintering ground first, settling in open areas and leaving the less suitable habitat for late arriving males. Why males don't migrate sooner is not clear, but perhaps there is no point because they would only be kicked out of the best territories by late arriving females!

## Territories and density in winter

Territorial behaviour is difficult to study in winter, and most of what we know comes from studies of kestrels. They seem to be largely territorial in winter, individuals or pairs fiercely defending their ground from intruders. Most of the fighting takes place in September and early October as the newly independent young create territories in the gaps between existing territory-holders. These fights can be very aggressive, the combatants sometimes tumbling to the ground and grappling with their talons. I once caught a bird just after it had finished such a fight and found several spots of blood where its opponent's talons had punctured the skin.

The more birds that settle, the smaller the average territory size. When voles are abundant some territories may be less than 100 hectares (250 acres), but they can be five times this size when food is scarce. Once the settling period is over there is little overt aggression because neighbours seem to respect their territory boundaries. However, if a territory-holder dies or leaves, its neighbours will quickly move into the vacated space, expanding their territories to do so.

The decline in density in winter is most obvious in upland areas because many birds move away or die. In sedentary populations there is a more gradual decline through the winter, probably due to mortality. In these populations, breeding numbers will mainly depend on how many birds survive in the area over the winter. In migratory populations, however, there is a rapid increase in numbers as birds arrive in early spring, and breeding numbers depend mainly on how many are able to settle.

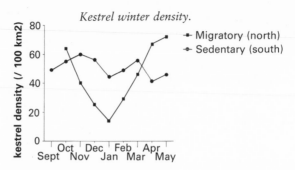

*Kestrel winter density.*

kestrel density (/ 100 km2)

80
60
40
20
0

Sept Oct Nov Dec Jan Feb Mar Apr May

→ Migratory (north)
→ Sedentary (south)

*The graph is based on counts I made during winter in Scotland ('north'), where kestrels were largely migratory, and in England ('south'), where they were sedentary. Mid-winter densities in Scotland were less than half those in England, but spring densities were higher as migrants moved in to take advantage of the abundant voles.*

## Hobbies: winter holidays in the sun

Little is known about what happens to hobbies in winter, nor about wintering populations of North American peregrines in Central and South America. Wintering hobbies are seen in small numbers over much of West Africa, but are most common in the southern savannas. Here they hunt flying insects such as swarming termites, grasshoppers and locusts, sometimes gathering in large numbers to feed with lesser kestrels or red-

*Hobby in Africa.*

footed falcons on swarms flushed by bush-fires. Insects are abundant after the rains, and hobbies follow the seasonal rain-fronts northwards in East Africa. They are one of the latest summer migrants to return to Britain, staying in Africa until mid- to late April to ensure that food is available when they reach their breeding grounds.

*Merlins often winter on the coast.*

# Kestrel mates

I once radio-tracked a pair of kestrels during winter in east England. They had partly overlapping territories, and would meet several times each day to sit together and preen their feathers. A favourite spot was a large horizontal branch of an ash tree. The pair roosted separately – he on the nearby church and she on the side of a windmill about 500 m away. Most of the day was spent hunting separately for beetles or earthworms on pastures, voles from patches of rough grass or small birds. During a prolonged bout of snow, however, they were forced to rely solely on birds, especially song thrushes and redwings, which became easier to catch as they weakened through starvation. The pair bred together for several years and wintered on the same territories until the male died and was quickly replaced.

# Pesty pesticides

Some of the peregrine populations most affected by pesticides have been those breeding in the high Arctic of Canada or Scandinavia, where there is little pesticide contamination. The reason is that these birds spend the winter in places where pesticides are heavily used — North American birds in Central and South America and Scandinavian birds in Central and Eastern Europe. The same problem holds on a smaller scale for peregrines and merlins in Britain, which breed in the relatively uncontaminated uplands but may pick up pollutants if they winter on farmland or beside estuaries. In theory, hobbies ought to be vulnerable to this problem because they winter in Africa where insecticides are often used to control pests.

However, pesticide levels in hobby eggs are relatively low compared with peregrines or merlins. Insects rarely accumulate much pesticide (they die quickly from a small dose), so hobbies may be less affected because they are mainly insectivorous in winter.

Insecticides might have an indirect effect by wiping out the food supply, and this would apply to other insectivorous falcons that winter in Africa, such as red-footed falcons and lesser kestrels. The latter species has declined drastically in Europe over the last two decades and problems on the wintering grounds are thought to be a possible reason. Blanket spraying from the air can kill all the insects in an area, leaving it barren for months afterwards.

# Obituaries: mortality

Something I am frequently asked when lecturing on kestrels is, 'How long do they live?' This seems a straightforward question, but the answer is more complicated than it appears. If I say that the longest-lived kestrel recovered in the British Ringing Scheme was fifteen years old when it died, the audience might go home thinking that all kestrels live to about that age. But this was one bird in over 3,000 ring recoveries, and very few kestrels ever reach that age. In fact, most kestrels die within a year of leaving the nest, so the *average* life-span is between one and two years. But this is also misleading because it is biased by the poor survival of juveniles. The answer I usually come up with is something like, 'If they survive to adulthood, the majority of kestrels live between two and five years.' Not exactly succinct, but probably near the truth.

How do we know this? The figures derive from the hard work put in by amateur bird-ringers and professional ornithologists over the last half century or so. Year after year they find nests and diligently ring the chicks,

*Less than one in three kestrels survive their first year of life.*

sending the details of where and when to the folk at the ringing office, who collect and store the reports of any birds that are subsequently recovered. These reports not only give clues about the bird's movements, but often describe how the bird might have died and when. Some reports will be too vague to tell exactly when the bird died, while others are of injured birds that are subsequently released. The rest show how old birds are when they die, and accumulating such records over many years reveals what proportion of the population dies at a particular age. From this it is relatively simple to work out the probability of an average bird dying or surviving at a given age.

Although our knowledge is incomplete for all the four British falcons, the best estimates suggest that peregrines have the highest survival rates and merlins the lowest. This ordering follows size, and is just what you would expect — elephants live longer than mice and ostriches longer than wrens! The longevity records depend strongly on how many birds are ringed and how long this has been going on. The oldest known British peregrine to date is sixteen years, only a year beyond the oldest kestrel. However, there are almost ten times more recoveries of kestrels, and I suspect the peregrine record will rise as more recoveries accrue.

## What kills falcons?
Life in the falcon world is rough, tough and dangerous. People who send in reports of ringed birds sometimes say how the bird died; to judge by these reports, falcons come to grief in all sorts of circumstances. Death can come suddenly from a speeding car or the barrel of a gun, slowly from starvation or pesticides, or ignominiously from falling into a water trough! The problem with these reports is that they tend to highlight the most obvious or bizarre ways of dying, and many birds are simply recorded as 'found dead'. What is more, ring recoveries themselves may not be a representative sample. After all, up to 96 per cent of ringed falcons die without being found, and those that are found are likely to be the ones that die near humans — flying into windows or hit by cars — rather than those that crawl under a bush to die in some remote wilderness.

One of the chief causes of death that is likely to go unnoticed is starvation. For many years the research station at Monks Wood near Huntingdon has been asking people to send in any dead birds of prey they find, whether ringed or not. The corpses are carefully autopsied (not a pleasant task if the bird was dead for some weeks before it was found and was then delayed in the post!) and the cause of death ascertained wherever

# Survival rates

Scientists use ring recoveries to calculate 'age-specific survival rates', another case of jargonitis that simply means the chances of getting through another year of life at a particular age. Imagine the ringing office has 1,000 recoveries of kestrels ringed as nestlings. The year they were ringed is recorded, so the date they are found gives their approximate age. A histogram of the number alive at any particular age would show a high mortality in the first year:

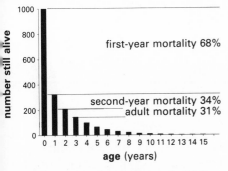

In this typical sample, only 320 of the 1,000 chicks ringed made it

to their second year, and 680 (68 per cent) died. Of the 320 survivors, 210 (or 66 per cent) were alive a year later, and 110 (34 per cent) had died. At any particular age, the proportion dying gives the mortality rate and the proportion surviving gives the survival rate. Unfortunately, you need to ring a lot of chicks to ensure you recover enough older birds to give a reasonable estimate of their survival rate, and our information is much better for kestrels than for the other species.

The data that are available suggest that falcons are similar to many other bird species in having a much higher mortality among juveniles than among adults. Once kestrels reach three years their chance of survival has improved from less than 35 per cent to nearly 70 per cent The high attrition of young falcons is part of the process of natural selection that ensures only the most able birds survive to breeding age.

possible. Since 1963 over 600 kestrels have been examined, and many of these show signs of being starved. This is particularly true of juveniles during autumn and early winter, when they first become independent, and after prolonged cold weather.

Another 'hidden' cause of death revealed by autopsies was associated with slow poisoning by pesticides such as dieldrin or DDT. These cause internal bleeding, and kestrels with these symptoms had higher than average concentrations of one or both these chemicals in their livers.

Adults were particularly susceptible, possibly because they lived longer than juveniles and so had more chance to accumulate the poisons. Overall, about 13 per cent of deaths between 1963 and 1979 were due to pesticides, but the level was much higher in the 1960s and early 1970s before the chemicals were effectively withdrawn from use. In recent years, levels of pesticides in kestrels have fallen, as have the number of haemorrhaged birds found. The same is probably true of peregrines and merlins, though the number of carcasses examined is much smaller than for kestrels.

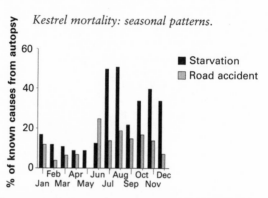

*Kestrel mortality: seasonal patterns.*

*Autopsy of kestrels sent to Monks Wood shows seasonal patterns in the cause of death that reflect the vulnerability of recently fledged juveniles to starvation and traffic accidents in their first six months of life.*

Accidents are a frequent cause of death reported for kestrels, particularly collisions with cars. The proportion of road-casualties among kestrel ring recoveries has risen sharply in the last thirty years, doubtless reflecting the increased volume and speed of traffic. Kestrels are often seen hunting beside roads, and sometimes fatally misjudge the speed of oncoming vehicles. This happened to a male kestrel that was handed in to me a few years ago by a distraught motorist. It seemed the falcon had caught a large blackbird right beside the road, and tried to carry it away before the car approached. Alas, his extra payload proved his downfall, and he just failed to clear the front bumper.

The good news is that deaths due to human persecution seem to have declined over the same period, though some of this may be more apparent than real. It has been illegal to kill falcons since 1954, so guilty parties, even if they bother to report a ringed bird, are unlikely to admit how it died. Once again, I had a graphic illustration of this from a radio-tagged kestrel, this time a female I had followed for several weeks. One day I found the signal had become very weak, and was not moving. After a frustrating search I finally found her – shot and stuffed down an old rabbit burrow. The trigger-happy culprit obviously hadn't realized the implications of that tiny transmitter. Such depressing incidents are fortunately rarer than they used to be, and shot birds account for less than 5 per cent of kestrel recoveries and 4 per cent of merlins.

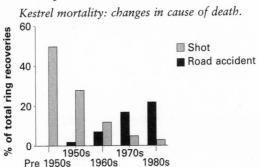

*Kestrel mortality: changes in cause of death.*

*National ring recoveries show how kestrels have become more prone to road accidents and less likely to be shot over the last forty years.*

# Diary of a Victorian bird-lover

*Just how much our attitude to killing falcons has changed can be judged by looking at the writings of Victorian naturalists. Many of them had a great love for wildlife, but saw nothing wrong in shooting birds to add to their collection. Take this account published in 1863 by Robert Gray, the secretary of the Glasgow Natural History Society:*

*'There is nothing in the possession of an ornithologist of greater interest to him than the well-preserved skins of those birds he himself has captured. Nearly every specimen recalls adventures by "flood or field" and presents memorable pictures . . . The following observations on the Merlin have been suggested to me by three fine specimens in my collection. They were shot by myself. One, a young bird, was cut down in a juvenile foray amongst a covey of partridges, probably his first infringement of the game laws; another disregarded my fowling-piece at thirty yards after lifting a barn-door duckling; while the third was killed as he seized a towering*

*snipe, and fell with a splash, prey in hand, into the marsh whence the prey had risen. As they lie on the table before me they carry my mind to distant horizons . . .'*

I particularly like the description of the merlin that 'infringed the game laws' — one has the distinct feeling that Mr Gray would have had no compunction in letting fly at human poachers with his fowling piece!

# Peregrines as pests

Wildlife has had a long and intricate association with humans in Britain, a fact well illustrated by the changing fortunes of our falcons. Whether deliberately or unintentionally, we have dramatically influenced the fate of these raptors; that they have survived our attentions is a tribute to their resilience and adaptability. The pressures facing falcons are highlighted in peregrines, which have suffered the extremes of problems that affect all the other three species in some form or another. For humans, direct contact with peregrines is usually in connection with leisure activities: for us it is often a question of sport, but for them this becomes a matter of life and death.

Things probably went well for peregrines until the last century. Medieval falconers may have taken a lot of birds, but they doubtless lost many back to the wild, and probably reared some chicks to adulthood who would otherwise have died. The age of game-rearing heralded an intense period of persecution. In some areas bounties were paid for dead raptors, and one Scottish estate recorded 98 peregrines killed from 1837 to 1840. Not all keepers were so efficient however, and some were positively tolerant, so there were often birds around to make up for losses. Some keepers would kill pairs on their beat every year, only to find them replaced the following spring. Indeed, some birds were replaced within a few days by non-breeding peregrines that came in to fill the gap created in the breeding population. Nonetheless, the continued killing must have made peregrines unnaturally scarce in some areas.

Another nineteenth-century pastime that caused problems was egg-collecting, peregrines getting more than their fair share of unwanted attention by virtue of their attractive eggs. This accounted for enormous numbers of clutches, some fanatics removing all the eggs from every pair in their patch, year after year. When Derek Ratcliffe came to measure shell thickness in peregrine eggs he was given access to hundreds of clutches in the drawers of museums and private collections. Most were taken over the last hundred years or so and were only a fraction of the number stolen because many of the early collections were lost.

The peregrine's fancy for pigeon has brought it into conflict with those who fancy pigeons for quite different reasons. Pigeons have been kept for food and decoration for hundreds of years, as evidenced by the medieval dovecotes you can still find in some villages. Racing pigeons came into fashion at the end of the nineteenth century, when the railways made it feasible to transport birds long distances from their lofts. This provided a weekend meals-on-wings service for peregrines which they readily accepted. Some well used peregrine nesting ledges are knee-deep in old pigeon rings. Not unnaturally, such a sight tends to raise the ire of some pigeon-keepers, who have on occasion wreaked revenge on the peregrines by destroying eggs or chicks. Such destruction has been sporadic, and nothing like the scale of that of gamekeepers or egg-collectors. Nonetheless, it was one more turn of the screw on the increasing pressure on peregrines.

Another point of conflict with peregrines arises from their use of tall cliffs for nesting. The growth in popularity of rock climbing has meant that many previously isolated crags now swarm with orange hats, ropes and pitons every weekend. Some peregrines adjust to the company quite well, but others are forced onto less suitable cliffs or may desert their eggs if they have already laid.

All these conflicts between peregrines and humans continue today, though on differing scales to the past. Peregrines are regularly found shot, and eggs and chicks still go missing. As recently as 1990, pigeon-fanciers are thought to have killed peregrine chicks at an eyrie in south-west England. But even at the height of these problems, peregrines were able to maintain reasonable numbers and a wide distribution around the country. But they could not cope with the agricultural pesticides used in the 1960s, and it was this purely inadvert side-effect that nearly caused their demise. Why?

The previous chapters of this book have shown how peregrines are relatively long-lived birds that may breed at the same site for several years in succession. Because of the restricted number of places they can nest, young birds must wait until older ones die in order to breed. But peregrines can fledge up to four or five young in a year, so there are normally lots of birds looking for somewhere to breed. Many of these will

# The other Battle of Britain

Pigeons were used to carry military messages during World War II, and peregrines threatened the lines of communication by eating the messengers. This was deemed treasonous behaviour by the Secretary of State for Air, and in 1940 the peregrines were sentenced

to death. The worst problems were along coasts, where it was feared that falcons might intercept carrier pigeons released by air-crews who had crashed at sea. So while troops sweated and died in the deserts of North Africa, and gallant RAF pilots held the Luftwaffe at bay, dedicated bands of peregrine bashers set to work with shotguns and ropes. It's estimated that as many as six hundred birds may have been killed throughout the country, though the effects were most noticeable along the Cornish and Devon coasts, where peregrines were all but wiped out. Fortunately technology replaced the pigeon and the need for killing soon passed. This incident probably would have had little long-term effect on peregrines if it had not been for the advent of DDT, which arrived on the scene just after the war and put a halt to the peregrine's recovery. The return to the south-west coast had to wait until the 1980s, when pesticide levels had declined sufficiently to allow the species to recolonize its former haunts.

die without doing so, and there is a high natural wastage. This means there is a certain amount of 'slack' in the system: remove the odd adult and another is likely to take its place. Furthermore, killing eggs or chicks has less effect than you might imagine because those young that do fledge are then more likely to survive to breed. Although in no way justified, the losses due to gamekeeping, egg-collecting and disturbance have normally been so sporadic that enough chicks were fledged to ensure breeding numbers were maintained.

But the widespread deaths of adults from pesticides were more than the system could take. When older birds died, immatures took their place. But they are poor breeders, and success was reduced anyway by egg-breakage resulting from DDT. So the stock of non-breeders diminished until there were no birds left to fill the gaps. Cliffs that rang every year to the cries of peregrines fell ominously silent. It is a sobering thought that these chemicals, applied in small amounts well away from the peregrine's nesting areas, did more damage in ten years than the persecutions of the previous hundred.

# Living nichely together

Although our four falcons are all predators built to a similar design, they have specialized in different lifestyles, or 'niches'. This allows them to co-exist in the same areas by minimizing direct competition for resources. The separation in lifestyles is partly a matter of size and partly to do with what they eat.

Peregrines are considerably larger than the other three species and because of this they generally eat larger prey, live longer, take longer to reach breeding age and produce fewer young per breeding attempt. This size-trend is apparent in other birds of prey and reaches an extreme in large eagles, vultures and condors. These birds live for many years, usually rear a single chick at a time and may not begin to breed until they are at least five or six years old. Their lifestyle is geared to raising a few young carefully, rather than churning out lots of offspring that have little chance of survival.

The very large raptors, such as the Californian condor, have such low breeding rates that they can at most fledge only one chick every other year. This is adequate provided that adults live long enough to breed many times. But they cannot compensate for increased adult mortality by producing more young quickly and have become the dinosaurs of the bird world, unable to cope with the rapidly changing conditions in their native

Mothers day at Mrs Condor's ...

habitats. Peregrines are relatively long-lived, but they are fairly prolific breeders for their size. They seem to get the best of both worlds, which may explain why they were able to quickly recolonize their former haunts once pesticides were banned.

Our other three falcons are more similar in size, and the differences in their ecology are largely related to what they eat. Merlins are bird-eaters that have a somewhat similar distribution to peregrines. However, their much smaller size ensures there is little direct competition for food, and they nest in very different sites to peregrines. Provided they keep out of the way, and avoid ending up as a peregrine dinner, they are able to share the same range as their larger cousin.

Kestrels take a wider range of prey than the other falcons, and also have a wide range of nesting sites. In some areas, this might bring them into competition with merlins, especially if they are using crow's nests and eating skylarks or meadow pipits. But the latter are secondary prey, taken mainly in summer when they are most vulnerable. Kestrels are primarily vole-eaters, so they are more likely to compete with owls, especially long-eared owls. In my Scottish study area, both long-eared owls and kestrels fed mainly on voles and nested almost exclusively in old crow's nests, which were in high demand. The owls bred earlier than kestrels and may have prevented some pairs from breeding by exhausting the supply of nesting sites.

Hobbies and kestrels are approximately the same size and their distributions overlap in southern Britain. However, they eat very different

... Mothers day at Mrs Peregrine's

*Peregrine over a nesting cliff.*

foods, and hobbies have more exacting nest requirements. In the areas where I worked in England, hobbies nested exclusively in old crow's nests, while most kestrels used tree holes. Hobbies feed on flying insects or creatures such as swallows and bats that eat flying insects, food that is rarely taken by kestrels. Each falcon is adapted to exploiting its food supply most efficiently. Kestrels can experience big variations in prey numbers from one year to the next as vole numbers fluctuate. They can exploit good years by breeding early and raising large broods. Hobbies are adapted to a food supply that is rarely super-abundant and that does not increase until late in the year. They are never as thick on the ground as kestrels and have to be content with breeding late in the season and rearing small broods.

# Falconomania

If this book has whetted your appetite for falcons there are several ways you can find out more. At the end is a list of books that give more details about falcons or birds of prey in general. But you may want to get closer to your subject than the pages of a book.

**Where to see falcons**
The easiest way of seeing falcons close up is to visit a bird of prey centre. You are guaranteed success and most places will have several species on display. With luck you may see falcons being flown by expert falconers. Some of the larger centres include the National Birds of Prey Centre, Newent, Gloucestershire, and the Hawk Conservancy, Wendover, Hampshire.

You might find all these captive birds rather tame stuff and would rather see the real thing in the wild. For kestrels this simply means keeping your eyes peeled in the right sort of habitat. The other species are more difficult to find, though there are some peregrine eyries that have organized public access, such as the one at Symonds Yat in the Wye Valley, Gloucestershire.

**Organizations**
The foremost national ornithological societies are the Royal Society for the Protection of Birds (The Lodge, Sandy, Bedfordshire SG19 2DL), which deals with all aspects of bird conservation, and the British Trust for Ornithology (The Nunnery, Nunnery Place, Thetford, Norfolk IP24 2PU), which organizes surveys, ringing and publishes research papers. The Hawk Trust (c/o Zoological Society of London, Regent's Park, London NW1 4RY) is devoted specifically to birds of prey, captive and wild, and sponsors research and conferences. The same function on an international scale is taken by the World Working Group on Birds of Prey (156 Bolton Gardens, London SW5 0AL). At the other end of the scale, local ornithological societies usually organize field trips and lectures, and members can be an invaluable source of information about falcons in your area.

# Build a box

If you have access to suitable trees or buildings you might try putting up nestboxes for kestrels. These can be sited anywhere that kestrels live, though farmland or parks with nearby rough grassland might be best. Although kestrels can be remarkably tolerant of humans, your best chance of success is somewhere quiet, away from dwellings, footpaths or picnic areas. Make sure you have permission to erect a box if the land is not your own.

Boxes need to be at least 3 m (10 feet) up, placed in a tree or on the side of a building. Access should be easy with a ladder, to make checking easy, but hard otherwise, to deter would-be thieves. Kestrels like sitting in the sun, so face the box south or south-east. The design varies, those for trees are usually oblong and open at the small end (Type A), while those for buildings are sometimes open along the longer face (Type B). The important thing is to ensure that the inside remains dry and is large

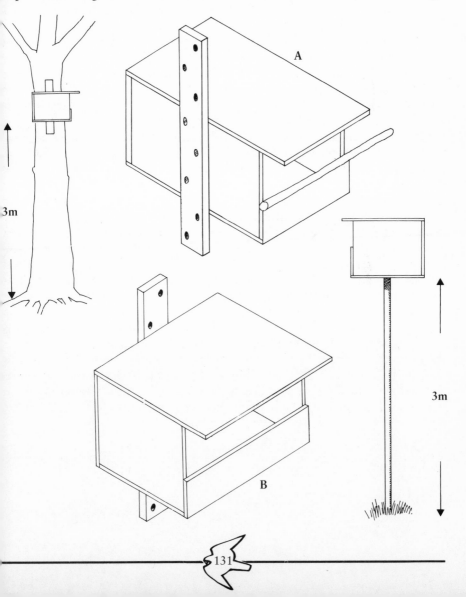

enough to accommodate a full brood. You will need to put some material in the box with which the birds can make a scrape. I have found kestrels nesting in empty boxes, but the eggs rolled around and soon broke. It is better to use light, peaty soil rather than sawdust or sand, which tend to dry out and blow away. I made a point of checking my boxes in early spring to ensure they had a good layer of material. Boxes need to be in place by March, and preferably a few weeks before if the wood has been preserved. Details of a variety of nestboxes are available from the Hawk and Owl Trust and the BTO.

If you live in an area with more conifer than deciduous trees you might have more success with artificial crow's nests. These are made of wire netting, formed into a basket and lined with twigs followed by grass, moss and finally soil. They need to be sited above the canopy with an open view, but not exposed to the elements. Against the trunk of a tree on the edge of a wood is a good site.

Nestboxes can be spectacularly successful in areas that have a good food supply but no nesting sites. In one reclaimed polder in Holland, boxes were mounted on poles and set out in a grid, about 300 m apart. In two years, kestrel numbers increased from 20 pairs to over 100 after boxes were erected in the intervening winter. Even where birds have natural sites, they may prefer boxes if they give better shelter and protection from predators. Kestrels do not need time to 'get used' to the box before they will occupy it. I have known pairs move in within twenty-four hours of a box going up! It depends mainly on how many natural nest sites are available locally: if there is lots of good hunting habitat (such as rough grassland) and few sites, kestrels could use your box in its first season. Otherwise, it's more a matter of chance and patience.

You could visit your boxes from mid April onwards, looking for signs of occupation (fresh white droppings, pellets or the remains of prey) or for the birds themselves. Visits will not disturb the birds provided you do not stay at the nest too long and avoid the laying and hatching periods. Remember, it is illegal to visit the nests of the other three species of falcon without a licence, and it is illegal to take eggs or chicks from any species' nest.

# Now read on . . .

Some books which give more details about falcons include:

Cade, Tom, *The Falcons of the World* (Collins, London, 1982). Covers all the 38 species of falcon individually, with a general introduction and many superb colour plates by Nigel Digby.

Ratcliffe, Derek, *The Peregrine Falcon* (Poyser, Calton, 1979). The definitive work on peregrines, written by someone with a life-long experience and devotion to peregrines. A good read as well as informative.

Village, Andrew, *The Kestrel* (Poyser, London, 1990). Based on my studies of kestrels over 14 years in Scotland and England, this book also includes information from many other studies in Europe and elsewhere.

There are numerous books that deal more generally with raptors, some of the best include:

Brown, Leslie & Dean Amadon, *Eagles, Hawks and Falcons of the World* (Country Life Books, London, 1968). Although rather dated, this is still a standard work, and has recently been reprinted in a single volume.

Newton, Ian (editor), *Birds of Prey* (Merehurst, London, 1990). A very useful introduction – lots of photographs and illustrations combined with an easily read but scholarly and up-to-date text.

Newton, Ian, *Population Ecology of Raptors* (Poyser, Berkhamsted, 1979). This book has had a major impact on the study of raptors over the last ten years and is a must for those wanting a detailed and scientific approach to all aspects of raptor ecology.

If you'd like to try your hand at some pellet analysis you might find the following booklet useful. Although aimed at owls, the information applies equally well to kestrel pellets.

Yalden, Derek, *The Identification of Remains in Owl Pellets* (The Mammal Society, Reading, 1977)

# Index

If you have enjoyed this book, you might be interested to know about other titles in our **British Natural History** series:

**BADGERS**
by Michael Clark
*with illustrations by the author*

**BATS**
by Phil Richardson
*with illustrations by Guy Troughton*

**DEER**
by Norma Chapman
*with illustrations by Diana Brown*

**EAGLES**
by John A. Love
*with illustrations by the author*

**FROGS AND TOADS**
by Trevor Beebee
*with illustrations by Guy Troughton*

**GARDEN CREEPY-CRAWLIES**
by Michael Chinery
*with illustrations by Guy Troughton*

**HEDGEHOGS**
by Pat Morris
*with illustrations by Guy Troughton*

**OWLS**
by Chris Mead
*with illustrations by Guy Troughton*

**POND LIFE**
by Trevor Beebee
*with illustrations by Phil Egerton*

**RABBITS AND HARES**
by Anne McBride
*with illustrations by Guy Troughton*

**ROBINS**
by Chris Mead
*with illustrations by Kevin Baker*

**SEALS**
by Sheila Anderson
*with illustrations by Guy Troughton*

**SNAKES AND LIZARDS**
by Tom Langton
*with illustrations by Denys Ovenden*

**SQUIRRELS**
by Jessica Holm
*with illustrations by Guy Troughton*

**STOATS AND WEASELS**
by Paddy Sleeman
*with illustrations by Guy Troughton*

**URBAN FOXES**
by Stephen Harris
*with illustrations by Guy Troughton*

**WHALES**
by Peter Evans
*with illustrations by Euan Dunn*

**WILDCATS**
by Mike Tomkies
*with illustrations by Denys Ovenden*

Each title is priced at £6.95 at time of going to press. If you wish to order a copy or copies, please send a cheque, adding £1 for post and packing, to Whittet Books Ltd, 18 Anley Road, London W14 OBY. For a free catalogue, send s.a.e. to this address.

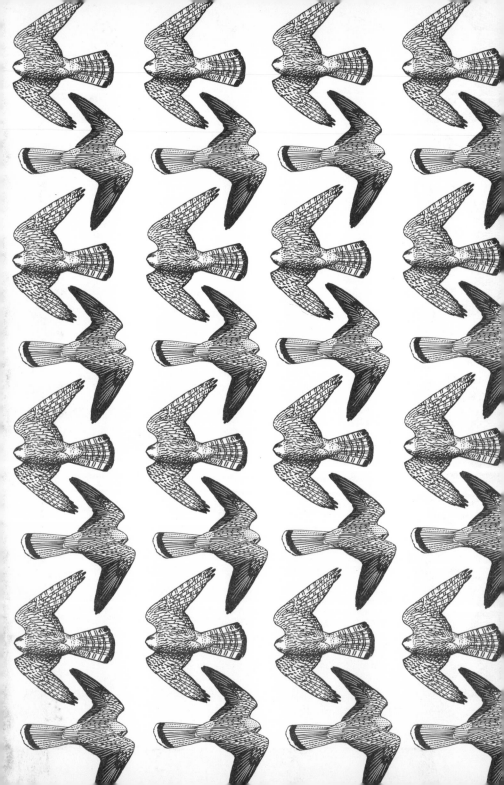